The British Horse Society

Riding
Manual

BARRON'S

The British Horse Society

Riding Manual

Margaret Linington-Payne M.A. (Ed.) BHSI

BARRON'S

First edition for the United States, its territories and dependencies, Canada,
and the Philippine Republic published 2008 by Barron's Educational Series, Inc.

Published by arrangement with HarperCollins Publishers Ltd
© HarperCollins Publishers 2007

All inquiries should be addressed to:
Barron's Educational Series, Inc.
250 Wireless Boulevard
Hauppauge, New York 11788
www.barronseduc.com

ISBN-13: 978-0-7641-6112-4
ISBN-10: 0-7641-6112-1

Library of Congress Control No. 2007931260

Created by: SP Creative Design
Editor: Heather Thomas
Designer: Rolando Ugolini

Photography
All photography by Rolando Ugolini with the exception of the following:
The British Horse Society: pages 184, 185 and 186
Margaret Linington-Payne: pages 26-27, 28-29, 84-85 and 164-165

Color reproduction by Dot Gradations, UK

Acknowledgements
The publishers would like to thank the following for their help in compiling this book:
Brampton Stables, Brampton, Northamptonshire, and Chris and Jo Bargmann

Printed and bound by Imago, Singapore

9 8 7 6 5 4 3 2 1

Contents

	Foreword	6
	The British Horse Society	7
1	Choosing a riding school	10
2	Preparing to ride	20
3	Your first lesson	32
4	The basics	54
5	Progressing	68
6	Tacking up and untacking	80
7	Refining your riding skills	98
8	Hacking out	110
9	Learning to jump	118
10	What if something goes wrong?	140
11	Looking after horses	156
12	What next?	176
	Useful addresses	188
	Glossary	189
	Index	191

Foreword

Riding is a really enjoyable sport and one of the fastest-growing leisure activities. You do not have to be young and really fit to ride - riding can be enjoyed by people of all ages, and it has so many positive benefits for us all. It is not only a marvellous way of getting out into the countryside and making new friends, but it is also a very healthy pastime, enabling you to live a healthy lifestyle in an increasingly sedentary society.

This book will instruct novice riders as well as more experienced people who are coming back to riding after a long break. It can also help existing riders to refine their skills and further their knowledge. As well as advising you on choosing the right riding school and instructor for you, there is expert advice on how to learn new skills and build on your confidence. There are also useful suggestions on how to progress once you feel competent, as well as what to do if things go wrong. Throughout the book, you will find many practical tips and reassuring suggestions on improving your riding skills, which take into account that learning to ride correctly is no easy task.

The British Horse Society is world renowned for its training structure, standards and system of professional qualifications and we are pleased to be associated with this excellent book. Within the following pages, there is something for everyone, whether they are learning to ride or fine-tuning their equestrian skills. The specially commissioned color photographs are particularly useful and informative in comparing good and poor practice, and the step-by-step instructional sequences will help you to overcome problems and progress with greater ease. The text is straightforward and easy to follow, making it relevant to all horse owners and riders.

Noel Edmonds
President, The British Horse Society

The British Horse Society

The British Horse Society was founded in 1947 when The National Horse Association decided to join forces with the Institute of the Horse and Pony Club to work together for the good of horses and riders. Membership of The BHS now stands at almost 65,000. In addition, there are 38,000 members of affiliated Riding Clubs.

As a registered charity, membership is vitally important to The BHS. Subscriptions enable the charitable objectives of the society to be met: promoting the welfare, care and use of horses and ponies, through the encouragement of good horsemanship, and the improvement of horse care and breeding. The British Horse Society represents all equine interests.

Access and rights of way

The U.K. has witnessed a dramatic change in the law that applies to off-road riding and carriage driving. Scotland has seen the introduction of the Land Reform (Scotland) Act 2003, allowing the right of responsible access for non-motorized users. Open Access has been introduced into England and Wales through the Countryside and Rights of Way Act 2000, although, sadly, only for walkers. The 2026 cut-off date requires all historic routes that were in existence prior to 1949, which are not yet recorded on the definitive map, to be registered, or they will be lost forever.

The Society's Access workload has grown in direct relation to the increase in demand. The Society's network of over 170 Bridleway Officers and 130 Affiliated Bridleway Groups effectively targets rural and urban access, and The Society is in consultation with Highway Authorities and other access organizations. The DEFRA (Department for Environment, Food & Rural Affairs) commissioned British Horse Industry Strategy aims to increase access to off-road riding and carriage driving. The Access Department and its volunteers are working hard to achieve this, together with our partners in the Equestrian Access Forum.

The Society is intrinsically involved with the additions of promoted off-road routes. All these routes are key initiatives of the Ride-U.K. project, which was launched by The BHS in 2000 with the vision of creating a network of riding and driving routes throughout the U.K.

Breeding and welfare

Another important aspect of the society's work is carried out under the breeding and welfare banner. However much The BHS does for the rider (and that includes non-members), its prime duty is working for the well-being of the horse. The Society's aim is to prevent neglect and cruelty before it ever takes place. In other words, educating and advising owners, particularly new owners, on correct management practices can nip potential problems in the bud. Over 90 BHS county Welfare representatives, coordinated by the Welfare Department at Stoneleigh, support and advise horse owners throughout the country. As the eyes and ears of The Society, they are in an ideal position to identify horses that are suffering and advise their owners.

BHS Welfare represents over 40 breed societies, which are affiliated to The BHS Horse and Pony Breeds committee. Active BHS participation on the National Equine Welfare Council, DEFRA subcommittee meetings, and Horserace Betting Levy Board (HBLB) committee meetings helps ensure the future well-being of horses in the U.K.

Safety

The BHS Safety Department is involved in every aspect of equestrian safety, representing all riders. The Society works closely with the Department for Transport and, as a direct result of their campaigning, the Highway Code includes specific advice to all who take horses on the road. Work with the County Surveyors Society has led to joint guidance being issued to Highway Authorities and those responsible for road surfacing. Liaison with the Ministry of Defense led to considerably more attention being given to the safety of riders through their review of helicopter activity.

The BHS Riding & Road Safety Tests take place throughout the U.K. and Eire with some 4,500 people each year learning to ride safely on the roads. Every county in the U.K. has a BHS Road Safety representative who works alongside The BHS Safety Department to ensure safer riding on the roads for all.

A wealth of information is available on safe equipment for horses and riders, particularly hats and body protectors, with representation from The Society on many committees, including BSI and BETA, where decisions are made regarding safety equipment for riders and their mounts. Working closely, and in partnership, with other safety-related organizations, The BHS Safety Department ensures that no aspect of equestrian safety is overlooked.

Training and education

The BHS has a large Training and Education Department, which handles over 12,000 inquiries each year. It administers a wide range of examinations, ranging from the Progressive Riding Tests for recreational riders through to a full professional qualification structure. Qualified instructors work to ensure that horses are trained and ridden sympathetically. The BHS believes that the public should be able to expect both a high standard of teaching and safety from riding instructors, and it has created a Register of Instructors to meet this need.

Since 1961, The BHS has run a scheme for the Approval of Riding Schools. Establishments that offer sound instruction in riding and horsemanship and whose premises, facilities, and animals are properly looked after are given The BHS "seal of approval." There are approximately 950 BHS-approved riding establishments in Britain and abroad. The system provides a useful guide for newcomers, with details of each riding establishment published in

Where to Ride. The British Horse Society also has an approved livery yard scheme up and running, to encourage livery yards to set high standards for their clients.

This vital work is coordinated and administered from The BHS headquarters with its permanent staff of 82. In April 1998, The BHS HQ moved to Stoneleigh Deer Park, Kenilworth (see page 190).

So how is it all done?

The Society is governed by a board of Trustees who oversee the work, funded largely by membership subscriptions. The national headquarters at Stoneleigh is supported by a network of regional and county committees – the hard-working and enthusiastic volunteers without whom The Society could not operate. Representative volunteers offer expert advice at regional and county levels in the fields of equine welfare, access and rights of way, and road safety, but committee members have the ability to represent the horse world on any subject. The committees are supported by Regional Development Officers who are full-time employees of the society.

Anyone who would like to support the work of The BHS can contact the membership department through The BHS web site at www.bhs.org.uk.

Chapter 1

Choosing a riding school

Now that you have made the decision that you want to learn to ride or pick up the skill again, you need to find a good riding instructor or riding school that will suit your requirements. Riding schools vary greatly in their size, location, and the facilities that they offer.

Your goals

First, decide what your goals are for your riding and what you want to get out of it. Within the two basic riding styles—English and Western—there are several riding disciplines to choose from for pleasure or serious competition. For example, Western riding, popular throughout the United States, but especially so in the western states, includes reining, roping, barrel racing, and rodeo events. In the English riding style, you may want to consider pursuing forward seat (also called hunt seat) riding if you're interested primarily in jumping, fox hunting, or cross-country eventing. In saddleseat equitation, used for gaited horses, the English-style cut-back saddle doesn't place the rider's position as far forward on the horse as in the hunt seat discipline. Dressage, another English-style discipline that has rapidly gained popularity in the U.S. within the past few decades, offers an excellent foundation in classical riding, which will benefit you in any equestrian sport or discipline that you may later decide to pursue. Many riders explore several disciplines before settling on a favorite. If you want to become competent enough purely to hack out or trail ride safely and enjoy the countryside, you should consider if it is worth learning to ride at a riding school where they do not hack out, as you will have to move on once you are a more competent rider. On the other hand, a riding school that concentrates solely on instruction may get you up to your required standard more quickly.

Even at a really busy riding school, the horses and ponies will be cared for, and health and safety will be a priority.

Points to look for

• The staff should be welcoming and friendly. They must be prepared to show you around and, if possible, will allow you to watch a lesson in progress.
• All areas of the stable should be clean, neat, and tidy.
• The horses should look well groomed, healthy, and content.
• The atmosphere should be welcoming and there should be an air of efficiency about the place.

A well-run riding school will ensure that all the areas, including riding surfaces, are maintained to the highest standards. Surfaces should be flat and never dusty.

13

Indoor schools

Not all riding schools have an indoor arena. This will not affect the quality of instruction, but it may influence whether or not you will want to ride regularly, whatever the weather!

Your nearest riding school may not be right for you, so phone a few centers before you visit to see if it fulfills your requirements and see how customer-friendly the staff are. Visit the center to get the feel of the establishment and discuss your needs before booking your first lesson.

Ask the staff about the school's organization of riding lessons and how they assess potential clients. You need to feel comfortable about the riding establishment, and confident that the staff will have your

The horses in a riding school should appear alert but well-mannered, and their stalls should always be clean and tidy.

best interests at heart. Ask about the staff's qualifications. Find out what discipline is the primary focus of instruction at the facility. Ask if you can observe a couple of riding lessons for a better idea of what to expect for your own first lesson and to discern whether you can cope with the teaching style. Some instructors yell like drill sergeants, while others take a gentler approach. Choose an instructor who makes you feel at ease and confident, who emphasizes safety, and who explains riding theory and principles clearly. You also want someone who will encourage you to challenge yourself, but not pressure you into trying something you're not ready to do.

Your instructor should be sympathetic and adapt his coaching methods to suit your goals and understand that you may not achieve a classically correct riding position, no matter how hard you try.

Many people do not feel comfortable with much younger instructors. If you feel like this, mention it on your first visit to the school, as you will need to have confidence in the person teaching you or you will not be able to relax, and your progress as a rider will be hampered. If, after a few lessons, you still do not feel you are achieving a rapport with your instructor, discuss this with the relevant person. There is no shame in not being able to get along with an instructor. The riding school may be able to change your teacher. Or you may need to investigate other facilities.

Riding lessons, whether they are taken in an indoor or outdoor arena, should always be well structured, enjoyable and interesting as well as safe.

Many novice riders feel safer if they start to learn on the lead rein. The close proximity of a teacher can give you confidence and lead to quicker progress.

What to look for

Look at the horses, stables, and paddocks while you are being shown around the yard, and take notice of how friendly and alert the horses appear. There may be one or two who are not as friendly as others, but generally they should seem relaxed and inquisitive. Always ask if it is acceptable to stroke them, and please do not offer them titbits over the door. If every visitor to the stables feeds the horses, it leads to them looking for food, biting, and kicking the doors. Consequently, many riding schools have a rule that horses may not be fed any titbits. A carrot given to a member of staff to be put into a horse's evening feed may be an acceptable compromise.

Look over the stable doors and check whether the horses' stalls are clean and tidy. There are many different forms of bedding for horses, but they should all be regularly "mucked out," i.e. the droppings are taken out throughout the day.

An alert but friendly horse shows he is well cared for and happy in his work. A "kind eye" is essential for a riding school horse. He should look calm and not frightened. His eyes should not appear as if they are "out on stalks."

Although these horses look happy, healthy, and generally well groomed, there are a lot of weeds that need to be kept under control to ensure quality grazing.

Fields and fencing

In some riding schools, the horses and ponies live outside in the fields when they are not working, although they may well be tied up in stalls when they are waiting to work. This is acceptable as long as the horses cannot reach each other to kick and bite. Take note of how well maintained the fences and fields are when you are being shown round. Fences should be secure and safe, and fields should not have noticeable areas of droppings, which are left to rot down, nor should there be large amounts of weeds in well-maintained paddocks. As with the stable yard, everything should appear safe and well cared for.

Is expensive best?

On your first visit to any riding school, you also need to discuss the cost of different types of lessons. These can vary a great deal, depending on the riding school's location, overhead, staff costs, and the facilities that are offered. The cheapest may not always be the best, but, on the other hand, the most expensive may not be either! You need to decide on your budget and then choose the school that you feel will suit you best within that price range.

This field is better maintained than the one shown above, as there are fewer weeds, and it is also securely enclosed with safe post and rail fencing.

Booking your first lesson

So you have decided on a school that has the right atmosphere and facilities for you. What is the next step? You need to take the plunge and book your first riding lesson. There are several different ways in which you can start your riding education, and the route you choose will depend on your individual preferences and what you can afford. Your riding school will advise you.

Private lessons

The first option is for you to have private lessons. These are probably the quickest and easiest way to learn to ride, but they can be expensive. You will have a teacher on a one-to-one basis and will be given individual assistance.

For your first few lessons, it is a good idea to book 30-minute sessions, so that your body does not get tired and your mind does not become overloaded with too much new information.

Probably the best way for you to start if you are a complete beginner is to have a lesson in which you are led around the arena, either by the instructor or by an assistant. However, as you start to feel more confident, you will be able to take more and more control of the horse.

Lunge lessons

In a lunge lesson, the teacher attaches the horse to a long line and stands fairly still while the horse makes a circle around him or her. The teacher also holds a long whip to encourage the horse to move forward. This kind of work is very hard, both for the horse and the rider, so a half-hour lesson is usually the maximum. Although it may seem unlikely that the teacher can keep the horse under control in such a manner, a good school horse will be accustomed

A lead rein lesson means that you do not have to worry too much about controlling your horse. Note the neckstrap around the horse's neck, so you can hold on if you feel unsafe, without balancing on the horse's mouth.

When you feel a little more confident, lunge lessons will ensure that you progress relatively quickly. You will work harder than on the lead rein and can concentrate on your riding position.

to being lunged and will be obedient. Once you have gained some confidence sitting on a horse, then a series of lunge lessons will help you to progress quickly with your position, balance, and skill.

Class lessons

Some riding schools may suggest that you join a class lesson when you start learning. The advantage of learning this way is that you can see that everybody else is having the same problems as you and can share the experience together. Class lessons will help you to build friendships with people who have the same interests as yourself. Another benefit for some beginners is that the concentration involved is not so great as in an individual one-to-one lesson.

Group lessons are usually of one hour's duration, so you may find this rather a long

session until you have ridden a few times. The number of people in a group lesson can vary – anything from three to about eight riders. Obviously, the smaller the group, the more attention you will receive from your instructor.

Some people feel that they do not want to do their initial learning in public, so class lessons will not be right for them. A group lesson can be a little intimidating if you do not understand the terminology that is used by the teacher to control the ride. If you are returning to riding after a long break, then the riding school may suggest a few individual lessons to brush up your skills before joining a group lesson at an appropriate level. If you are a complete beginner, you may wish to take a number of private lessons until you feel confident, and then move into a group session.

Chapter 2

Preparing to ride

Riding is a great way to take exercise, make some new friends, and see the countryside. Now that you have taken the plunge and decided to have some lessons, you will need to ensure that you are safely equipped. You will also find that the fitter you are, the easier your lessons will be and the quicker you will progress. This chapter contains essential advice on getting ready to ride.

Clothing

When you have your first riding lessons, you may not want to go to the expense of purchasing all the clothing and equipment you will require straight away. It is usually better to wait a little while until you are sure that riding is the right sport for you and that you want to progress further. The riding school will be willing to offer you advice as to what equipment you need and what is suitable for you to wear while not compromising your safety and comfort.

Riding helmets

Most riding schools have riding helmets for hire, which must conform to current safety standards. However, it is advisable to purchase your own helmet after taking a few riding lessons.

Always go to a tack shop where someone with equestrian experience can help with your selection. They will ensure that you purchase a helmet that not only fits you correctly but also offers your head the maximum amount of protection in a fall.

This horse is ideal for lunge lessons. He is a sturdy cob who looks sensible and keen to do his job. The rider is appropriately dressed for a hot day.

If you feel that in the future you may want to compete in one of the many riding disciplines that are now on offer, you should check first with the rules of that discipline to see what their requirements are.

Replacing helmets

If you do fall off your horse and land on your helmet, replace it as you can never be sure how much damage has incurred on impact. Wearing it because it seems undamaged is a false economy; it is better not to compromise your safety.

Styles of riding helmet

Riding helmets are now available in two very distinctive styles: traditional velvet hard helmets (as shown here) and skull caps (see page 25), which are usually covered with a colorful silk or velvet covering. Generally, there is no difference in the amount of protection that both types of helmet offer, and which style you choose is a matter of personal preference rather than safety. For cross-country riding, however, many people tend to favor the skull cap type.

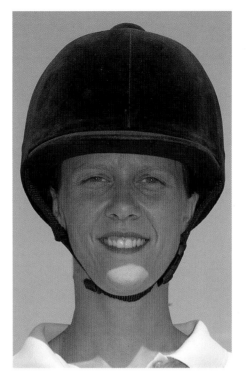

Always check the American Society for Testing and Materials and Safety Equipment Institute standards inside the helmet before buying. If you are unsure whether a helmet is the right size for you, ask the staff in the store for advice.

Help is at hand

The riding school will be willing to offer you help and advice about what is suitable to wear while not compromising your safety and comfort.

This riding helmet fits the rider well. Note how it is positioned correctly on her head.

This helmet is sitting too far back on the head and will not give protection.

This helmet is at an angle and will not protect the rider's head in a fall.

The chin strap of this helmet is far too loose and is unsafe for the rider.

23

Jewelry

Jewelry should not be worn when you are riding, although a watch and a smooth ring are acceptable. Other items may get lost or could even injure you.

Jodhpurs and breeches

For your first few lessons, you can wear some comfortable trousers rather than investing in jodhpurs. The trousers should not be too loose and baggy, or they will cause friction. However, if they are too tight, there is a possibility of them splitting when you mount and sit astride the horse! Do not wear jeans because the seam on the inside is bulky and will chaff your legs.

Once you have decided that riding is definitely right for you, it is sensible to purchase a pair of jodhpurs, which are designed specifically for riding. They are not only comfortable to wear but will also protect your legs. Alternatively, you can wear breeches, but these are shorter than jodhpurs as they are always worn with long riding boots. They are also much more expensive than jodhpurs.

Shirts and jackets

You need to wear clothing on your upper body that is suitable for the conditions in which you will be riding. It is always wise to keep your arms covered, so that if you are unfortunate enough to fall off they will be protected. However, many people do wear short-sleeved tops in summer if the weather is very hot. Clothes should not be loose and flapping as this may frighten the horse. A jacket in winter and a short-sleeved shirt in summer will fit the bill.

You may need to wear an overcoat if you are riding outside or throughout the winter. Make sure it is the right length, so you don't keep sitting on it, which can be extremely frustrating when you are riding.

Footwear

The correct footwear is an essential part of your equipment, and not only for riding. Horses are not aware of where you are putting your feet when you lead them, and thus they may inadvertently tread on one of your feet should you not be in the correct position. Therefore you need to wear strong footwear that will provide you with some protection at all times.

Sneakers are totally unsuitable and unsafe as they give no protection to your feet and have no heel. A small heel is crucial as it will stop your feet from slipping through the front of the stirrup should anything untoward occur. Heavy-ridged soles are also not suitable – they can trap your foot in the stirrup. If the tread is very deep then it is hard to control your foot in the stirrup.

Which boots are best?
The ideal footwear is a pair of jodhpur boots or long riding boots. You probably will not want to purchase these straight away, so a strong pair of shoes is a sensible substitute for your first few riding lessons. Lace-up shoes are better than those with buckles, which can catch on the stirrups. As previously mentioned, the sole of the shoe should not be too thick.

When you decide to purchase a pair of boots for riding, it is down to your personal preference whether you choose to wear short jodhpur or long riding boots. Long boots do offer more protection for your legs and can stop stirrup leathers chaffing and pinching. They come in leather and rubber – rubber ones are more affordable and are totally acceptable for leisure riders.

Gloves

Riders are always advised to wear gloves, preferably close-fitting ones. They will not only protect your hands from the reins, preventing rubbing, but will also help to keep them warm in winter.

This novice rider is ill equipped for a riding lesson, and a safety-conscious school would not allow him to ride. His trousers are too baggy and he is wearing sneakers. Although he has a helmet, it is set too far back on his head, and he has no gloves.

25

Get fit for riding

Riding is a sport and, although you do not need to be very fit to go out for a trek or a gentle hack in the countryside, if you want to progress with your skills, you do need to consider your level of fitness and the muscles you use the most when riding.

Use your muscles

Many people who are just starting to learn to ride are under the misconception that all you have to do to ride is just to sit on a horse. However, nothing could be further from the truth. Riding is an extremely strenuous activity, which helps you to use a large number of muscles in your body, and this is why you may feel a little stiff or sore after your first few lessons. The fitter and more supple you are, the fewer problems you will experience in this area, although a favorite saying of many riding teachers is: "No pain, no gain!"

The exercises

There is a wide variety of exercises that you can undertake to help you to develop your suppleness and thereby make your riding lessons easier and more worthwhile. Initially, you may feel very stiff and unable to perform the exercises easily. However, don't give up – if you can find just a small amount of time each day to practice them, you will gradually become more supple and this will really help you when you start to ride. Do not try to push yourself too hard too quickly, or you could do yourself real damage. If you are in any doubt about your health or level of fitness, consult a medical practitioner before starting.

1 Standing up straight with your weight evenly distributed across both your feet, turn your head as far as you can to the right. Hold for up to 10 seconds, then look to the front.

2 Now repeat the exercise to the left. Check that you can turn your head the same distance in both directions – left and right. If one way is easier, work more on the stiffer side.

Starting off

If you are unaccustomed to exercising, it may be worth contacting your doctor before you embark on any kind of exercise program to discuss the best way of starting to get fit.

This exercise is excellent for stretching out your calf muscles. Place your hands on a wall and take your left leg back. Lean your body weight on the wall and then hold for up to 15 seconds. Repeat with the other leg.

To stretch your inner thighs, sit up with your legs straight. Make fists with your hands and place them on the floor behind you. Open your legs, lean forward slightly, and push down on your fists. Hold for 20 seconds.

1 This exercise helps to make the hip flexor muscles more supple. Kneel on one knee and stretch up tall, with your arms above you. Hold for up to 10 seconds.

2 Lean forward and rest your fingertips on the floor. Hold for up to 10 seconds and then return to the original position. Repeat with the other knee in the same way.

Take it easy

When you start doing the exercises, do take care not to work too hard. You should listen to your body and build up gradually, stretching a little more each time. By putting aside a few minutes every day for these exercises, you will soon find that you become more supple.

1 This exercise helps the triceps muscles and can be done sitting or standing. Take your right arm up and drop your hand down behind your head between the shoulder blades.

2 Take your left arm around your head and hold your right elbow. Hold for up to 10 seconds and then repeat the exercise on the other side with the left arm.

1 This exercise helps flexibility and loosens your spine. Stand with feet slightly apart, stretch your arms out at shoulder height and then twist as far as you can to the right.

2 Without moving your feet, twist as far as you can to the left. Repeat this exercise several times, working hard in order to achieve an equal rotation in both directions.

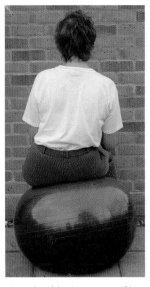

To aid core stability, sit on a Swiss ball with your weight equally distributed across both your seat bones.

Here the rider has more of her weight on the right seat bone. Notice how her shoulders are not level.

The rider has collapsed her left hip and slipped to the right, putting more weight on the left seat bone.

If you are sitting correctly with your weight distributed properly, you should feel both your seat bones equally. Your shoulders and hands should be the same height.

Using a Swiss ball can help with your core stability and balance. In a good position, your shoulders should be relaxed with your head directly above your spine.

What are your goals?

The fitter and more supple you are before you start riding, the quicker you will make progress. It really is worth making the effort to work on your fitness before you actually start to ride, although, of course, it all depends on what you want from your riding experience and how far you wish to go. Sit down and ask yourself: "What are my expectations from learning to ride?" You may not know at the beginning and these may change as you progress and find the sport increasingly absorbing. What may start as a desire to accompany a friend or a sibling may turn into an overpowering passion to learn more and even to become a competitive rider. You may even start off just wanting to be able to hack out on a sunny day but end up deciding that you wish to make a career out of horses.

Riding in a classical position

To enjoy your lessons and riding experience you need to have long- and short-term goals. You should discuss these with your instructor; what you hope to achieve could alter the way in which you will be taught. It is always better to try and learn to ride in a classical position as near as you possibly can. From a correct classical position, you can move on to most other equestrian disciplines and your horse will be able to work more easily for you. If, however, you know for certain that you will only ever want to have a quiet hack out, then it is not so vital that your position is totally correct. You must, however, always be in balance with your horse and not have to use your reins to stay on board. To be balanced, your weight must be, as near as possible, over the horse's center of movement, so that he can carry you easily.

Riding out on a warm, sunny day is enjoyable and an exhilarating experience that can be shared with like-minded people. Both horses and riders look happy here.

Contact with horses

It is sometimes a good idea to spend some time with horses before starting to learn to ride. If you have ridden in the past, no matter how long ago, you will probably already have a little "feel" for horses and will not be so worried about coming into contact with them. People who have no previous experience of horses may even find their size and behavior intimidating. Consequently, if you can spend just a few minutes with them – perhaps stroking them over a stable door, or watching other people ride or look after them – you will be a little more confident when you finally start riding. Horses are large animals and some anxiety is perfectly normal if you are not accustomed to being around them. Any contact you can have with them will help to overcome this fear.

Approaching a horse

Because horses in the wild are animals of flight they can be nervous. If they are approached by someone making quick, sharp movements, they will become more nervous themselves. If you can approach them calmly and confidently, this will ensure that you get off to a good start with your mount. You can only achieve this if you have a certain degree of confidence yourself. This will come with familiarity, so take every opportunity to approach a horse and try to make friends with him. If you are unsure of how a horse behaves, it is safer to do this from the outside of the stable door and not to go into his stall. Do not try to do this in a field; you could put yourself in a tricky position without even knowing it.

Observe and learn

If you get the opportunity, observe people who are confident with and knowledgeable about horses. Notice how they are always positive and purposeful when attending to a horse. Familiarity should never breed contempt when dealing with horses – they have brains and can think for themselves. Most riding school horses will be sensible, well-mannered and accustomed to having people around them who are unsure of the environment, but this does not mean that you can be complacent. Horses should always be treated with kindness and respect to encourage the growth of a positive, healthy relationship between the rider and horse. It will certainly be worthwhile and the respect will be mutual.

This horse and rider are showing mutual trust. The horse is happy and inquisitive, and the rider is positive without being threatening.

Chapter 3

Your first lesson

The day has arrived for your first lesson. If you have done your homework and chosen a riding school you feel confident about, then all should go well. Be prepared to listen to what you are being taught, and don't rush; take everything one step at a time. Horses are kind, helpful creatures who will do their best to accommodate you and will forgive your mistakes. Remember that you are taking up riding for fun, so relax and enjoy yourself.

Know your horse better

For your first lesson, your horse may be brought to the arena for you, but if you tell the staff that you want to get to know your horse better, they should take the time to show you how to approach your horse and lead him yourself.

Looking after a horse

Eventually, you should learn some basic stable management skills, which are always useful (see page 156). This helps you to start to understand the way in which a horse thinks, so that both of you will be safer together. Also, if you decide one day to take the huge leap and buy your own horse, you will need to know what skills are required to take care of him.

Horses in the wild

In the wild, the horse is a creature of prey, which means that he is constantly on the look-out for predators. Although he has excellent vision to the front and sides, there is a small area immediately in front of his head where he is unable to see.

As a creature of flight, he uses his

Stabling horses removes the opportunity for physical contact. In this barn, the horses can at least see each other. A good riding school will turn out horses regularly for exercise and social contact.

speed to get him out of trouble. Only when he is cornered and there is no escape will he fight, using his legs and teeth to good effect to protect himself.

Wild horses travel in herds for safety, forming bonds with each other. In the herd, there is a hierarchy and every horse knows his place within it. A horse may sometimes challenge this pecking order and may succeed in raising his status within the herd.

You may think all this has no relevance to learning to ride, but you need some knowledge of a horse's natural lifestyle and the way in which we compromise this when we domesticate him, so that you can understand his reactions to what he is being asked to do.

Horses are herd animals and they feel safer in the company of others. They will only relax and graze if they are not afraid, although one horse will be on guard.

This horse is showing a relaxed interest in his surroundings. He is not at all frightened and he appears to be quite confident with a good temperament.

35

Building a relationship

When we ride horses we must remember that in the wild a weight on their backs means that they have been attacked by a predator. Building up good relationships with horses by consistent handling and continual schooling means that they gain our trust and are prepared to accept us humans as dominant. Consequently, they look to us for support and guidance.

Starting to ride

When you have your first lessons you will be given a horse who is frequently used for novice riders. He will be able to help you out because he knows what is going to be asked of him, and he is not overly sensitive. The relationship that you build up with your first horse is one you will never forget. Therefore it is important that for the first few lessons you are always given the same horse so you can get used to his rhythm

Always take the opportunity to talk to your horse and pat him before you mount.

and obedience to the aids. You will then quickly become more confident and thus make better progress.

One thing you will quickly learn about riding is that every horse is different, and therefore riders continually learn to adapt and refine their skills. Even the best riders in the world are still learning – the process never ends! So you must be patient and keep on practicing – you will improve.

Some horses seem to sense what you want almost before you ask them while others take more persuasion. Just as with people, you will feel more comfortable with some horses than others. Learning to ride correctly is a long and sometimes bumpy road, but the rewards can be fantastic. You may even find yourself becoming obsessed with the desire to learn more as you continue to improve as a rider.

Once you are competent, there is no better feeling than riding out across open country on a well-schooled horse on a fine day. Riding with a friend is very enjoyable and also a good stress-buster after a hard day's work.

A healthy horse

A healthy horse's coat should appear shiny. His eyes should be bright and he should be alert and interested in what is going on around him. He should not be too fat nor too thin. This horse has all these traits and is well cared for.

Points of the horse

It is a good idea to try to learn the major "points of the horse." Your riding instructor may well talk about the withers or the hocks, for example, and, although they should point them out to you, you will be one step ahead if you are already familiar with the terminology and where they are located on the horse's anatomy. This useful illustration shows you the most important points. Spend some time looking at them and try to familiarize them; it will be time well spent.

Bay horses

The horse shown here is a bay with white "socks" on his back legs. A bay has a brown body (light or dark) with a black mane and tail. The bottoms of his legs are also black unless he has "socks" as shown here.

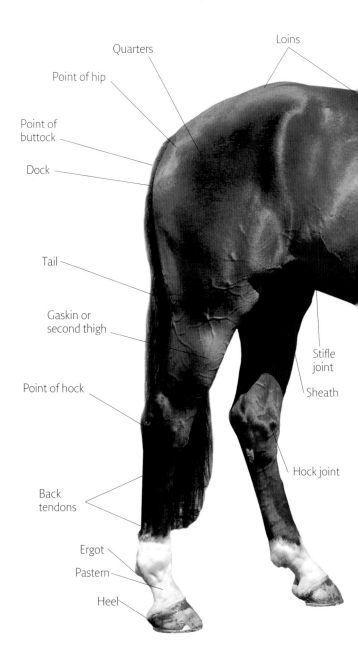

Quarters

Loins

Point of hip

Point of buttock

Dock

Tail

Gaskin or second thigh

Stifle joint

Sheath

Point of hock

Hock joint

Back tendons

Ergot

Pastern

Heel

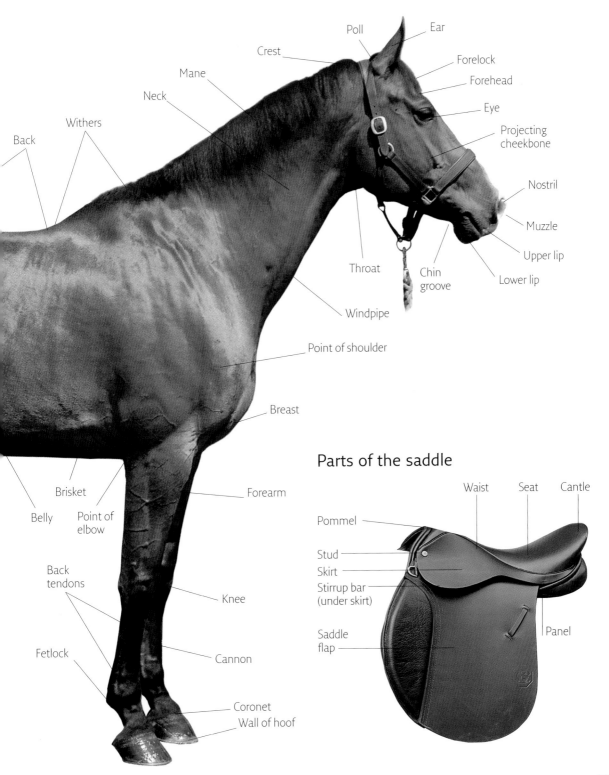

Poll

Ear

Crest

Forelock

Mane

Forehead

Neck

Eye

Withers

Projecting
cheekbone

Back

Nostril

Muzzle

Throat

Chin
groove

Upper lip

Lower lip

Windpipe

Point of shoulder

Breast

Parts of the saddle

Waist   Seat   Cantle

Forearm

Pommel

Brisket

Stud

Belly   Point of
elbow

Skirt

Stirrup bar
(under skirt)

Back
tendons

Saddle
flap

Panel

Knee

Fetlock

Cannon

Coronet

Wall of hoof

Picking out the feet

A horse should always have his feet picked out before he comes out of the stable, so he does not drag his bedding onto the yard. Your instructor will show you how to do this safely.

When leading a horse, always stand close to his shoulder and push him past you with a straight arm. This rider is safely positioned, but moving even closer back towards the horse's shoulder will ensure that she does not get her feet trodden on.

Leading a horse

The moment has come and you have arrived at the riding school for your first lesson. If you have already visited the school and booked the lesson in person, then you should have filled out the necessary paperwork. If not, you will be expected to do this before you start to ride.

Leading out of a stable

If you are given the opportunity to lead the horse from his stable to the arena, there will be somebody there to help you and to ensure that everything is safe. You will be escorted into the horse's stall and shown exactly what to do.

The horse may already be tacked up and may be tied up with a halter on over his bridle. The person with you will explain the routine for the riding school. The halter may well be undone at the horse's head and re-done up through the tie ring, or it may be untied at the wall, the halter then undone and taken out of the stable with the horse.

Leading guidelines

When leading a horse that is tacked up, always ensure that the stirrups are not flapping loose, so they cannot be caught on anything. Also, the reins should be taken quietly over the horse's ears, so that you have more to hold on to for security.

Traditionally, the horse is led from his left side – the "near" side. Horses should be encouraged to be led from both sides, but you will find it easier from the left. It is not a difficult procedure; just double the reins up in your left hand, and with your

right hand hold both reins behind the horse's chin. The only exception to this is if the horse is wearing a running martingale (see page 189), in which case you should not put the reins over his head as the martingale will pull down on his mouth.

It is sensible to be prepared and already wearing your riding hat and gloves. You will be safer and your hands will be free to lead your horse. Don't forget to talk to him.

This rider is ready to mount. The reins are back over the horse's head and the stirrups have been pulled down in readiness.

Secure the stable door

When taking a horse from a stable, it is important that the stable door is fixed back securely so that it will not be caught by the wind and then knock into either of you. You must ensure that you bring the horse straight out through the middle of the door to prevent him catching himself on the door. Do not attempt to turn him until his whole body is out of the doorway or you will inadvertently catch his hips.

Be confident

Once you are out of the stable, you should walk purposefully towards the arena with your horse. Walk to the side of him by his shoulder. If you get in front of him or try to pull him, he will back off from you. Also, you are less likely to get your feet trodden on if you are at the side.

Try and push the horse past you with a straight arm and be prepared to encourage him verbally with a brisk "Walk on." If you show you are nervous or not practiced at leading horses, he will not respond to you as well as if you give him confidence in your movements and tone of voice. The person who is assisting you may well be on the other side of him, ensuring that you are both safe.

Now you can see why your horse is often brought into the arena for you. To lead a horse well is a skill in itself, but one that is well worth learning so that you can start to build up a relationship with him.

This horse is being led out of his stall. Note how he is positioned in the center of the doorway, and the rider does not turn him until he has exited completely.

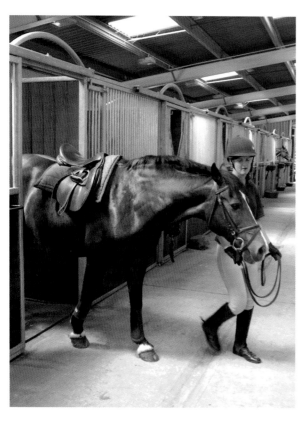

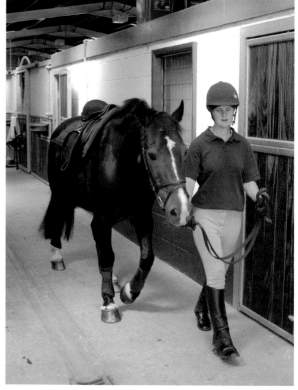

Checking the girth

Before you mount, you will need to check the girth and also adjust the stirrups to approximately the correct length. When checking the girth, always put your hand under the front of it. If you put your fingers under the back of the girth you will be rubbing the horse's hair the wrong way and may make him uncomfortable.

The girth should feel firm to your hand; if not, you need to lift up the saddle flap and tighten the buckles. You will probably find that the two girth buckles are done up on the first and third buckle straps. This is for sound safety reasons: the first and second buckle straps are usually attached to the saddle by the same piece of webbing and if the girth was attached to those and the webbing broke there could be a real problem. However, if they are attached to the first and third buckles and one piece of webbing breaks, you will still have one

buckle attached. By using two straps that are not positioned close together it can make everything less bulky under your thigh. Always ensure that you pull the buckle guard down over the buckles – this will also help to protect your leg.

1 Lift the saddle flap to check the girth; you may need to adjust the buckles to tighten it.

2 Make sure both the buckles on the girth are tightened equally. Your teacher will check, too.

3 Check how taut the girth is, and ensure the buckle guard is pulled down over the buckles.

Safety check

Before you mount, your teacher will check that your girth and stirrups have been adjusted correctly to ensure your and the horse's safety.

Stirrup length

If you check your stirrup length before mounting, you will not have so much adjusting to do once you are mounted. You will be secure in the saddle even if a slight change in stirrup length needs to be undertaken.

Checking the stirrups

The next thing you have to do is to check the approximate length of your stirrups, so they will not be far too long nor too short when you mount.

Adjusting the length

To alter the length of the stirrup, you need to pull down the buckle under the skirt of the saddle, take the tongue of the buckle out of the hole, and then move the buckle up or down to make it shorter or longer. Your teacher will show you how to do this correctly. Once this is done, you need to pull down the underside of the leather until you hear the buckle click on the stirrup bar. You must then go round the other side of the horse, changing hands and checking the other side.

Lift the skirt of the saddle and adjust the buckle (see left). Pull down the left stirrup with your right hand, keeping your left one through the reins. Put your right middle finger on the buckle and, with your left hand, take hold of the stirrup iron, and place it under your right armpit.

The rider's stirrup iron just reaches her arm pit, so the stirrup will probably be approximately the correct length when she is mounted.

This stirrup will probably be far too long for the rider when she is mounted. Notice how the leather has a loop in it.

Mounting

The next major hurdle is to get on your horse. Many riding schools encourage you to do this from a mounting block, which makes it easier for the horse, not just for you! If you mount from a block you are more likely to mount efficiently and there will be no damage to the saddle or horse's back. If you have brought the horse into the arena yourself, the first thing to do is put the reins back over his ears. Put your arm through the reins, so you have some control but leave both hands free.

How to mount

You will probably be given a demonstration of the correct way to mount. Whether you are mounting from a block or from the ground, the basic principles are the same.

Learn the terminology

In the horse world there is a new vocabulary to learn. The glossary on page 188 will help you to understand some of the terms, and we will discuss some more in this chapter. It is always useful to know the names of the parts of the saddle and bridle, so that you understand basic instructions, such as "tighten the girth" and "hold the pommel." These are things that you might be asked to do in your first lesson.

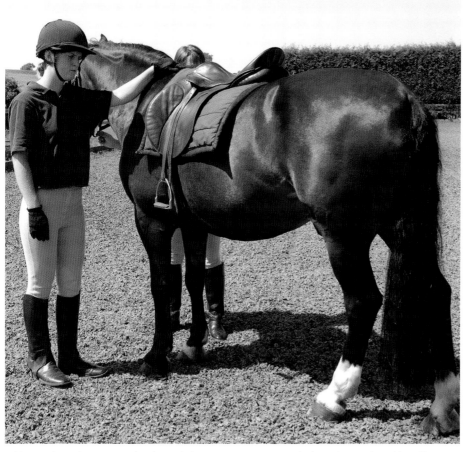

1 You need to take up your reins through the bottom of your left hand. Make sure the reins are not twisted and that they are not too long nor too short. If they are too short, there will be too much pressure on the horse's mouth and he will react by moving backward or fidgeting. If they are too long, you will not be able to stop the horse from moving forward while you are mounting.

Mounting from the ground

If you are mounting from the ground, once you have your left foot in the stirrup you need to spring once or twice on your right leg to give you momentum, and then spring up, passing your right leg over the horse's quarters before sitting down gently in the saddle.

2 Place your left hand on your horse's neck. If you are standing on a mounting block, make sure you are not standing in such a way that you are unable to see the horse's hindquarters.

3 With your right hand, take the back of the stirrup iron and bring it out toward you. Hold the stirrup iron, not the leather. The leather may look twisted but it will turn as you mount.

4 Put your left foot in the stirrup and push your toes down, so that you will not dig your horse in the ribs as you mount. Notice how this rider is just about to push her toes down.

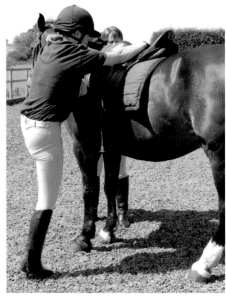

5 Reach for the waist of the saddle on the off-side. Swing your right leg clear over your horse's quarters and sit down gently in the saddle. Try to make the movement quick but controlled.

Mounting from a block

Horses have to get used to being mounted from a mounting block and feel happy to stand still and close enough for you to mount safely. Always make sure that you have checked the girth and stirrups before approaching the block.

It is more beneficial for your horse's back to mount from a block, so you should not feel awkward or embarrassed about using one. Some people even feel that they have failed if they are unable to mount from the ground, but this is far from the truth. The benefits for the horse and the saddle should always be your major consideration when mounting – not whether you feel foolish or less of a rider for having to use a mounting block.

1 Always make sure that the back part of the stirrup is turned outwards, in the same way as you do when mounting from the ground.

A "leg up"

When you have been riding for some time, you may be offered a "leg up." This is a skill that you will learn later on; it is not easy for a novice rider to perform.

2 When your left foot is in the stirrup, reach for the waist of the saddle and positively but gently push yourself up with your right leg.

3 Sit gently in the saddle with your weight evenly distributed. Ensure that you and the horse are comfortable before setting off.

Practice makes perfect

These basic skills are difficult to master at first. Your instructor will help you in the early stages and will check you have completed the tasks safely. The old adage that "practice makes perfect" is very true, and soon you will find that these tasks are second nature to you.

Check the girth again

It should become a habit once you are mounted to check your girth. Horses can learn the trick of puffing out their rib cage when you first do up the girth, and what felt tight before you mounted may now be rather loose, so check before moving off.

1 When you are mounted, check that the girth is correctly fastened. To do this, put both the reins into your right hand, lean down, and put the fingers of your left hand under the girth near your horse's elbow. It should feel taut with no large gap between the horse and the girth.

2 If the girth feels loose, leaving your left foot in the stirrup, bring your leg up on to the horse's shoulder. Lift up the saddle flap with your left hand and feel for the girth strap. Tighten both buckles, check that the buckle guard is in place, and then let the flap fall back into place.

3 Finally, you can bring your leg back into the correct position. You will need to check your girth again after you have been riding for a few minutes. This skill appears to be relatively easy, but to keep your balance and feel safe takes a lot of practice.

Altering stirrups while mounted

Once you are mounted, you may feel your stirrups are not the correct length. To alter them when mounted is a difficult skill to master, so the sooner you start practicing the better. Eventually it needs to be done by feel rather than by looking, but this comes only with practice. Your teacher may well alter your stirrups for you.

Stirrup loops

Some saddles have a keeper for the stirrup leather, but it is not necessary to put the leather through this loop as long as it is behind your leg. Sometimes putting the leather through the keeper will make it too bulky under your thigh.

1 To alter your left stirrup, put the reins in your right hand. With your left hand, pull the spare piece of stirrup leather up toward you, so the tongue comes out of the hole.

2 To make the stirrup longer, push with your foot onto the stirrup iron. Let the leather slide down until comfortable. With your finger, feel the tongue of the buckle back into the nearest hole.

3 Pull the underside piece of leather until you hear the click on the stirrup bar. This tells you the buckle is as high as it can be.

4 Put the spare piece of leather behind your thigh, so that it will not rub or pinch the skin of your thigh.

49

These hands are turned flat, so the thumbs are not uppermost. This makes for "heavy hands" on the horse's mouth.

These reins are being held incorrectly. The part coming from the horse's mouth is going through the thumb and index finger, making "heavy hands."

These reins are held correctly. They come up between the little and ring fingers and through the palm of the hand. The thumbs push gently on the reins to help stop them slipping.

Holding the reins

If you are a complete beginner, you may not hold the reins for the first part of your lesson. You may be asked to hold onto the neckstrap or the front of the saddle.

If you do hold the reins, hold one in each hand, so that they come up between your little and ring fingers, through the palm of your hand and out over the top of your index finger with your thumb pushed gently on the top. The spare end of the reins should be placed between the reins and your horse's neck, so that their weight does not press on to the rein and thereby be transmitted down to the horse's mouth.

Light and relaxed

Your hands should be in a position just above your horse's withers, 3–4 inches (7.5–10 cm) apart, and they should be level. Your hands and wrists should feel light and relaxed. Think of having a small bird in each hand which you don't want to squash to death but, equally, you don't want to fly away – this is the kind of feel you are trying to maintain with your hands on the reins. You can see that this is no easy task when there are so many other things to think about, and this is why some riding schools suggest that you do not hold the reins initially. It is important to remember that the horse's mouth is at the other end of the reins.

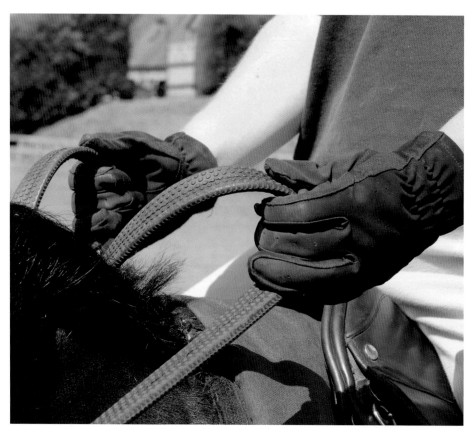

Your riding position

Your instructor will probably demonstrate to you the position that you should try to achieve when riding your horse. It is generally accepted that the "classical" riding position is the one that is currently taught and used. It has the advantage that you sit over the horse's center of motion, thereby making it easier and more comfortable for him to carry you. It also means that you can use all your riding "aids" efficiently (see page 56) and, eventually, unobtrusively.

The classical riding position

There are two invisible "straight lines" in the classical riding position. The first is a line that goes down the side of your body from your ear, through your shoulder, hip and heel. The second is a line that goes from your elbow, down the bottom of your arm and hand, along the reins to the bit in the horse's mouth.

You should be sitting centrally in the lowest part of the saddle with your weight equally distributed on to your seat bones. Your stirrups must be of the same length so that you do not lean to one side.

In the picture (left), the rider is sitting "square" with her weight equally distributed through both seat bones. In the picture (right), the rider has collapsed her right hip and slipped left. Both she and the horse look uncomfortable.

51

What are the aids?

These are the methods used to control a horse. There are various ways to give him information as to what we want him to do. These can be split into two types: natural and artificial.

• The natural aids are our seat, legs, hands and voice.

• The artificial aids are those we give to the horse with pieces of equipment. The most common are whips and spurs. You will not be using artificial aids until you have good co-ordination and balance. We will discuss these later on in the book (see page 144).

Stay in balance

A horse is not an armchair and you should not sit slumped with your weight at the back of the saddle. Although this may be more comfortable for you, the rider, it is much more difficult for the horse to carry you as you are "out of balance" with him, i.e. your weight is not positioned correctly over his center of motion.

Have you ever given somebody a piggy back? If they slip down your back, your immediate reaction is to push them back up so that it becomes easier to carry them. However, the horse cannot do this if your weight slips back and he has to suffer in silence. This may give him a sore back and will certainly mean that he is unable to perform at his best for you.

It is also incorrect to tip forwards and let your legs slip back when you are riding. This puts you in a very insecure position, and if the horse trips or moves suddenly you will inevitable land on the ground. You will also be unable to use your aids (see page 56) efficiently.

Achieving a good position

A good riding position is something that we are all trying to achieve and maintain. For many of us, however, it will not be possible to master a genuinely correct classical position, but for our horses' sake we should continually try to do so, and this is where the fitness exercises we perform off the horse (see page 26) can really help to improve our suppleness and thereby increase the likelihood of us achieving the dizzy heights of a correct classical position. Make some time, if possible, to practice them every day.

What to expect

During your first lesson you will probably spend a lot of time talking about your riding position and feeling the movement of your horse underneath you. You will probably be led round an indoor or outdoor arena on a leading rein and may stay in walk throughout. However, you may be given the opportunity to try a sitting trot.

If you start slowly and carefully, you will eventually progress faster once you have established your basic riding position. Do not be afraid to ask your instructor any questions that come to mind, or to tell him or her if you are experiencing any problems, so that he or she can help eliminate them.

Dismounting

At the end of the lesson you will need to dismount correctly. To do this, place both your reins in your left hand with a piece of the horse's mane. Take both feet out of the stirrups, then lean forwards and throw your right leg over your horse's bottom. Try to land on both feet, facing forwards, keeping hold of the reins.

Your instructor will then show you how to run your stirrups up the back of the stirrup leathers. You are now ready to take the reins back over your horse's ears in readiness for leading him back to his stable. Remember what you have been taught – to lead him from his left side, walking by his shoulder with your feet well out of harm's way. Your riding lesson is over and you have taken your first steps towards becoming a rider. You should feel exhilarated by the experience and that you have achieved something.

This rider is sitting too far back on the horse with her feet pushed forward. The position may feel comfortable for her, but it can give the horse a sore back. It is also more difficult for him to carry the rider.

Here, the rider appears to be perched on top of the horse. She is not balanced or relaxed and looks very insecure. If the horse trips, she is more likely to fall off.

53

Chapter 4

The basics

Now that you have learned the correct way to lead your horse, mount up, check the girth, and adjust the stirrups, the time has come to start using your aids to communicate with your horse and also to learn how to start, turn, and, most important of all, stop! To be able to coordinate your aids will take time and practice, but you will soon learn to use your seat, legs, and hands to pass on your instructions to your horse.

Using the aids

When you start using your aids you may be a little uncoordinated, and thus communicating with your horse could be difficult. The horse might not be sure as to what you require of him. He will probably know that you are a novice and are anxious and unsure about what is going on.

Always try to make your aids clear and positive, but not overly strong. It is better to use gentle aids first, and then, if your horse does not respond, you can be a little firmer. If you are too positive initially and your horse is very responsive, you may find yourself going faster than you want to.

Handling your reins

When you start riding, your reins frequently slip longer. However, this will happen less often as your riding improves and you maintain that gentle but firm feel on the reins that is so important (see page 50). As you become more relaxed, your arms will follow the movement of your horse more readily, so he will not take the reins from you.

Shortening your reins

Because you will frequently lose "contact" with the horse's mouth, you must become efficient at shortening your reins. The best way to do this is as shown opposite.

This rider is sitting in a basically correct classical position with her hands as a pair. A novice might find these stirrups a little long.

This rider has her left rein shorter than her right. Therefore her hands are not a pair and her horse is looking left.

The same length

You must always ensure that your reins are the same length. In order to do this correctly, you need to feel the weight that you have in each hand and also to make sure that the tips of your horse's ears appear level in front of you. If they are not level, then his head may be tilting and you will probably have one rein that is shorter than the other, thereby pulling his head one way all the time. This will make it very difficult for your horse to move forward correctly.

1 The reins are held correctly in both hands, but the rider feels the need to shorten them.

2 To shorten your left rein, put it through the thumb and first finger of the right hand.

3 Slide the left hand down the left rein until it is the length that you require.

4 Let go of the left rein with the right hand. To shorten the right rein, reverse the process.

5 Here the reins have been correctly shortened and the hands are positioned correctly.

Light hands

To become a good rider, you must work towards having sympathetic and light hands. Remember that at the other end of the reins you are holding a large lump of metal, which is in your horse's mouth.

Moving forward

The first aid you will learn is how to make your horse move forward from halt to walk. However, it is also very important for you to know how to slow down before you move off! This should give you more confidence.

Walking on

To ask your horse to walk on, "take off the brakes." You need to give a little with your hands toward the horse's mouth. Do not exaggerate the movement – do just enough to release any pressure on the mouth.

Now think of sitting up tall and give your horse a gentle nudge with both your legs. Think of using the whole leg and not just the lower leg from the knee downward.

Try to feel that your legs are staying in the same place near the girth to give this aid. It is far easier to move your legs back to do this, but this is incorrect and can make you tip forward.

If your riding position does not have the straight line down the side of your body (see page 51) and your lower leg is pushed too far forwards, your leg will not come into contact with your horse's sides and the leg aid will not be clear to your horse.

Using your legs correctly

Later on, you will need to be able to use your legs further back to tell your horse to execute more complicated movements. To use your legs correctly is one of the most difficult maneuvers for a novice rider. A good exercise is to place a football between your calves. Practice pushing your calves together to get the feel of the muscles that you need to use.

This rider is using her legs correctly on the girth to ask her horse to move forward.

This rider has moved her legs too far back to use to ask her horse to walk on.

Making your horse stop

To ask your horse to stop, think of sitting up tall, close your fingers around the reins, and keep your legs on your horse's sides. If your reins are a little too long and your horse does not respond, then bring your hands back toward you, keeping the straight line with your arms and down the reins. This means that your hands come almost toward your stomach, not down toward your horse's withers.

When you become more competent as a rider and you can keep a consistent rein contact, your hands will not need to move in a backward direction. It may seem strange to keep your legs on your horse's sides, but this will help him to step up with his hind legs into the halt.

This horse and rider are together in perfect harmony and are ready to move off.

Be relaxed

When a horse is walking, his head moves backward and forward. If your hands are light and not fixed, you will find that the horse will move them with this motion. This is good practice and shows that you are relaxed. Your horse will feel that he is not being restricted and he will be happy to keep walking forward. Initially, you may not hold the reins in your hands, but when you feel safe enough to let go of the neckstrap or the pommel, you will notice that your hands should move to and fro with the horse's motion if you are relaxed.

This horse has halted squarely, with his weight distributed equally on all four legs. This means that you can only see two legs when looking from the side.

Turning your horse

Now that you can make your horse start and stop, you also need to be able to get him to turn right and left.

Turning left

1 The first thing you should do is to look to the left. As you do this, open your left hand. Turn your wrist a little as well, so that you think toward the movement you would make with your thumb if you were a hitchhiker thumbing a lift.

2 Your inside leg needs to nudge a little in its normal position near the girth. If you can remember to do it, your outside leg should move back behind the girth and nudge a little. This outside leg movement becomes more important as you progress with your riding and wish to influence the horse more. However, as a novice rider, it may be one thing too many for you to think about at the moment. Don't worry; you just need to be aware that later on it will become important.

Turning right

To get your horse to turn right, all you need do is just repeat the instructions (left) but on the other side to the right.

As your horse turns in the direction you require, you can gently release the aids back to the "normal" position so that he realizes you want him to go straight.

These riders in a class lesson are all showing that they can turn their horses accurately and can keep them working around the outside track of the indoor arena.

What your horse feels

It is amazing how much your horse can feel the slightest movement you make. To be aware of how your upper body can influence him, sit upright in the bath with your legs out straight. Turn your upper body left and then right and feel how your seat bones scrunch on the bath. The horse can feel this through the saddle as well as the movement of your weight altering.

This rider is learning how to ride inside a riding ring. She will eventually be able to make her horse work around the outside or perform school figures.

61

Changes of rein

Your teacher should get you to practice turns, halting and walking on until you feel confident and understand how light the aids can be for the horse you are riding. Some of the turns you will be asked to do will involve you "changing the rein" in the arena, and there are many different changes of rein you can practice.

Walking

The walk is a four-time movement in which the horse puts one leg down at a time. The sequence of legs when he moves in walk is as follows: if he starts with the left hind leg, the left front leg will be the second beat, the right hind leg will be the third beat and the right front leg the fourth beat. As you get more confident, you will start to feel the movement of your horse's legs under you. This is something you can start to think about as your confidence increases. It is important to try to continually improve your "feel" of the way your horse moves underneath you. This will help you with your general control and eventually will mean that you can affect the work your horse does, so that you can help him improve the quality of his way of going.

1 The right hind leg is coming forward and is being put down to make the first beat.

2 The right fore leg is the next leg to move forward and be placed on the ground.

3 The horse's left hind leg is now moving forward to make the third beat.

4 The horse's left fore leg is brought forward to complete the sequence.

Trotting

When you feel confident about asking your horse to walk on, turn, and stop, you will be ready to learn to trot. There are two ways in which you can trot – rising and sitting. You should learn to do a small amount of sitting trot first, as it will give you the feel of the movement and will help you learn to rise. When the horse moves from walk to trot, the sequence of his legs changes from four beats to two. He does this by putting down diagonally opposite pairs of legs together with a moment of suspension in between (a short time when all four of his legs are off the ground).

Starting to trot

When you start to trot, hold on to the neckstrap or hold the front of the saddle; then if you feel unsafe, you will not be tempted to pull up on the reins and affect the horse's mouth.

1 The right hind and left front legs (with blue bandages) are moving forward together.

2 The left hind and right front legs (with white bandages) are moving forward together.

3 The sequence is repeated, with the blue bandaged legs called the left diagonal pair.

4 This is followed by the white bandaged legs, which are known as the right diagonal pair.

Armchair position

It is tempting to ride in what is known as the "armchair position." This is where you sit on the back of your bottom rather than on your seat bones. In this position, the small of your back collapses and you are behind your horse's center of motion, making you heavier and more difficult to carry.

The sitting trot

To sit correctly for a sitting trot, think of sitting up tall, lifting your diaphragm a little, and trying to stay as soft as you can through your hips. If you can achieve this, you will find that your horse will move you, and you will start to absorb the motion he gives you. If you can stay soft and relaxed, it will be much easier. Unfortunately, this is easier said than done, and many novice riders who feel a little anxious about learning to ride are consequently rather stiff. This means they are unable to absorb the movement and the process becomes more difficult, making them even stiffer.

This rider is practicing sitting trot on the lunge. She is sitting tall but is relaxed.

This rider is in the "armchair position" with her weight too far back and her feet forward.

Although this rider's stirrups are quite short, she is sitting relatively tall and soft.

Notice how the rider is holding on to the neckstrap to help her balance.

This is why you should practice your trot in short bursts, so that you can rest and readjust your position ready to try again. There is no secret in learning to ride – it is just practice, practice, and good teaching.

Good posture

Good posture is essential if you want to be a first-class rider. If you think of a skeleton, the spine is very slightly concave in the small of the back. This is how your spine should be when you adopt a good posture and, consequently, when you are out riding. You should be aware of your posture not only when you are riding but also at different times of the day, such as when you are driving, sitting at a desk in the office, relaxing at home, or walking. Try the traditional way of improving your posture by walking around with a book on your head for a few minutes a day – it will certainly help you with your riding position.

Rhythm of the trot

Think about the rhythm of the trot underneath you. Can you feel the one-two, one-two? If you can't, it is difficult to learn the rising trot, where you "post" up and down in the saddle in time with the rhythm. Try saying "one- two, one-two" out loud to ensure you feel the rhythm. Your teacher will tell you if you've done it correctly.

This rider is riding the trot across the long diagonal of the arena. She is relaxed and is in good balance. Her horse is thinking forward and listening to her, waiting for the next aid.

Correct technique

It is important to learn the correct technique for rising trot, so you can control your body and stay in rhythm with your horse. Resist the temptation of using your hands and reins to help you rise – your horse's mouth is at the other end of the reins.

The rising trot

To learn rising trot, you can start off by practicing standing up and sitting down in the saddle in halt. Firstly, stand up and see if you can balance and stay there. The secret of this is to keep your lower leg secure and your whole leg as near as you can in a straight line. This exercise is good for your balance, but it is not the actual technique for use in the rising trot.

When you start to practice your rising and sitting (still in halt) try to think of your hips coming a little forward as you rise. You will not need to go as high as you did when you try standing up. The secret is to try and control the coming down part and to sit softly down on to your seat bones and not to allow yourself to sit heavily on to the back of the saddle. If you do this, your lower leg will shoot forward and you

1 This rider has her seat in the saddle. She is preparing to rise on the next beat.

2 She is rising up here, although her upper body could be inclined a little more forward.

3 The rider now sits down again. She has not let her leg push forward.

4 She rises again. Her lower leg is secure but she is pulling up and balancing from her hands.

will be unable to continue to rise without pulling up on your hands.

To undertake the rising trot correctly is difficult and it needs a lot of practice. You will probably find initially that you will fall behind your horse's center of balance. If this happens, ask the person who is in charge of your horse to walk, so that you can correct your position: bring your leg back under you and sit up correctly again.

Do not worry if this takes you a long time, as it is better to get the technique correct at the beginning rather than having to relearn it later on. Once you are confident in executing the rising trot and do not have to use your hands to help you balance, you can start to use the reins and amalgamate the rising trot with control of your horse. Your skills are expanding already and are becoming easier to perform.

This rider is much more competent and is happily riding in rising trot out on a hack. Riding out on uneven ground can alter your horse's balance and rhythm and make rising trot more difficult.

Chapter 5

Progressing

Now that you are happy performing the rising and sitting trot and are able to control your horse in these paces, you can start to think about adding some refinements. There is always something new to learn in riding, and just when you feel that you have reached a level of competence in one skill, there will be another thing that you need to master to help improve your feel and riding ability. This chapter gives you advice on how to progress.

Diagonals in rising trot

To make good progress as a rider, you need to learn about your diagonals in rising trot. This name comes from the diagonal pairs of legs that your horse puts down as he trots. If you always sit on the same pair of legs your horse will start to brace himself for this and consequently will build up the muscles more on one side of his body than the other. You should sometimes sit on one diagonal pair of legs, and at other times on the other pair.

Fortunately, when we are riding in a school, we set a rule that says you should always do the sitting down part of the rising trot as your horse's outside front leg (and inside hind leg) are on the ground. This not only helps to balance the horse but also enables you to use your inside leg more easily to encourage him to use his inside hind leg.

When you are out hacking, there is no rule to be followed about which diagonal you are on. You should change frequently, however, so that you are not always rising on the same one.

Feeling the diagonals

Don't worry if you cannot feel yet which pair of legs is on the ground – as you make progress, this will come. For the moment, it may be easier just to look at your horse's outside shoulder, which comes back toward you as his front leg is on the ground. Consequently, if you are in sitting trot, you will see this shoulder coming back toward you and then you can start rising. This is one of the reasons why you should always start your rising trot with a few strides of sitting.

Some people find it difficult to work it out this way, so you could look at the inside shoulder and rise as that one is coming back toward you. It has the same result. If you keep looking to the inside, you can throw your weight too much this way and

Too heavy

A common fault with many riders is that they sit too heavily when they sit twice to change the diagonal. Being too heavy on your horse's back will upset your balance. When you sit twice to change the diagonal, try to think of keeping your shoulders forward a little, and do not allow the small of your back to collapse.

1 The rider is on the right rein in the arena and rising as the inside front leg is on the ground.

2 The rider then sits as the outside front leg is on the ground.

3 Look at the horse's leg bandages. The right diagonal pair are white and the left are blue.

4 The rider sits as the blue legs touch the ground and rises when the white legs are on the ground.

Wrong diagonal?

If you find yourself on the wrong diagonal, which can happen frequently, then you simply have to sit twice – or miss one up beat – and then you will be sitting on the correct diagonal (pair of legs).

thus disrupt both your balance and that of your horse. It is more difficult to throw your weight too much to the outside.

Changing the rein

If you think about it, you will be changing your diagonal frequently when you are riding in an arena as you will need to do it every time you change the rein. If you are going across the long diagonal, the best place to change the rein is just before you reach the letter you are going to. If, however, this is not convenient, then change it as soon as it is opportune.

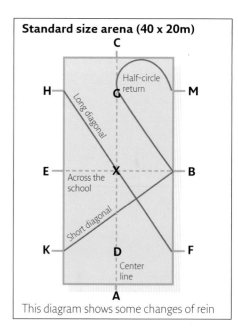

Standard size arena (40 x 20m)

C
Half-circle return
H — G — M
Long diagonal
E — X — B
Across the school
Short diagonal
K — D — F
Center line
A

This diagram shows some changes of rein

The rider is sitting on the inside diagonal pair of legs and rising as the outside diagonal pair are on the ground. This is incorrect and she needs to sit twice to change the diagonal.

Confidence

You may be thinking by now: "Am I making progress quickly enough or in a similar way to other novice riders?" It is important to remember that everybody is an individual and what one person finds easy may be difficult for another, and vice versa.

Group lessons

If you are having private lessons and you now feel ready to move on, it may be worth talking to your instructor to find out if this would be a good time to move in to a group lesson. You will not receive personal

This rider is riding the sitting down part of the rising trot quite well for hacking out, although her upper body should not be inclined any further forward.

For the rising trot, she needs to think of not rising quite so high. Once you have mastered the rising technique, you can become a little lazy and not put too much effort into the pushing up. Let the movement of the horse push you out of the saddle, then go a little further and control the movement down.

73

Attention to detail

Some riders worry that they are not progressing fast enough and there is too much attention to detail. However, in riding, your partner is a living animal and you need to do everything you can to take him into consideration. Attention to detail will ensure this and will also help you to build up a relationship with your horse.

tuition but you will see other riders having problems and be able to discuss all things equine with them. If you feel confident enough to make this step, then you are definitely making progress.

Build up gradually

Confidence is important in learning to ride, and this is also true of your whole equine experience. If you are over-confident, you may be tempted to try things that are beyond your limitations, which could lead to your downfall. However, if you have no confidence, you will progress very slowly and may even feel that riding is not for you.

A good teacher will build up your confidence gradually to help you improve your riding skills – the two go hand-in-hand. Even the best riders in the world will sometimes have twinges in their confidence, so don't worry about that. Just work within your limits until you feel that a new task has become easy and almost "second nature," and then you can move on to mastering more difficult skills.

Riding without stirrups

One skill that we all need to learn and which is excellent for improving our balance, position, and confidence is riding without stirrups. Your instructor may introduce a small amount of this as soon as she feels you are confident enough to cope with it. However, if it is undertaken too early, there will be little benefit. If the prospect of riding without stirrups horrifies you to the point that you become so stiff that you are unable to move, there will be no advantage in trying it.

Walking without stirrups

When you first ride without stirrups, you will only do it in walk. Once you take the plunge, you will probably feel that it is nowhere near as bad as you thought. Stirrups impose a discipline on your legs to keep them in the same place, and when you can get rid of them, you may find that you can soften your hips more easily.

In order to ride without stirrups, you will probably be asked by your instructor to: "Drop and cross" them. As in most aspects of being around horses, there are accepted ways of doing things. The conventional method is shown opposite in more detail.

Starting in halt

Initially, when you begin this exercise, it is best to do it in halt, so that you do not have to worry about what the horse is doing and keeping in balance with him. Make sure that you keep a contact on the reins in case your horse does decide that he wants to move. If so, you will be able to restrain him quickly and effectively.

Taking away your stirrups

To take away your stirrups, you must take both feet out and then pull the buckles down and away from the stirrup bar a short way. You can then put the stirrups over your horse's withers and rest them on the sides of his shoulders. Cross the right stirrup over first. We do this so that if you should happen to slip gracefully to the ground, you will only have one stirrup to uncross to remount. As you cross the stirrups over your horse's neck, turn the leather and buckle upside down so that they lie flat and will not rub your thighs.

1 After taking your feet out of both stirrups, pull down the buckles.

2 Cross the right stirrup over your horse's withers on to his shoulder.

3 Repeat the process with the left stirrup, so the leathers are crossed over the withers.

4 If the buckle is turned upside down, the leather will lie flat under your thigh.

Benefits

Riding without stirrups has three benefits for the rider: it improves your balance, deepens your seat, and lengthens your leg. It also boosts your confidence and, once you are used to it, you may prefer to ride without stirrups.

Relax your legs

Riding without stirrups is one of the best ways to improve your position and feel. If you do feel unsafe at first, then hold the neckstrap or front of the saddle with one hand. Do not be worried about asking your instructor to lead you until you feel safer. Try to relax through your hips and let your legs feel long under you. Think of bringing your leg back from the hip so that your thigh is as long and straight as possible. One of the reasons you should ride without stirrups is to lengthen your leg, and the only way you can do this is by straightening your thigh. So if you grip with your thigh and fix your hips, this is of no benefit. Bring your thigh back from the hip and then let your leg hang down.

With stirrups, the leg is short with the thigh at an angle of about 45 degrees to the hips. Compare to the leg position without stirrups.

Without stirrups, you can see that the rider's thigh is longer and straighter, and is in a good position for flatwork.

After working without stirrups, the rider is able to lengthen her stirrups in order to ride in a more classical position.

Some relaxing exercises

There are various exercises that you can practice regularly to help relax your legs.

• When mounted, circle your ankles both inward and outward – both legs together, then one leg at a time. This helps develop coordination and is good preparation for more advanced riding skills. Later on, you will have to do one thing with one leg and something else with the other – not easy when there is a horse underneath you.

• A good exercise, but one you should be careful about trying, is to bring your leg out to the side a little and then back from the hip and let it relax. At first, only do this a small amount – it really pulls at your hip joint and may well give you cramp. To help you to do this when mounted, practice the exercise below on the ground.

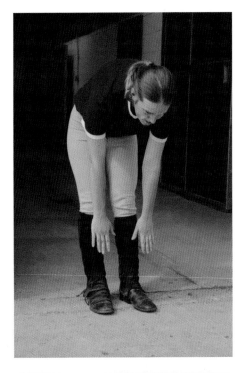

Reaching down toward your toes is a good exercise for stretching out your hamstrings. Don't overdo it. Keep practicing and you will see how you gradually get nearer to your toes.

1 Holding on to something for balance, bend one knee and lift your leg up as shown.

2 Slowly turn your knee out to the side, as far as it will go, but make sure you keep it high.

3 Lower the leg to the ground with the toes facing out, then repeat with the other leg.

Don't curl up

As humans, when we feel threatened we tend to protect ourselves by adopting the fetal position. Unfortunately, when riding this is one of the worst things we can do. The fetal position is rounded, and we need to sit tall and proud to help maintain our balance. If you feel unsafe when trotting without stirrups, try to sit tall rather than collapse, and only trot a few strides at a time.

Loosen your hips

To become a proficient rider with a riding position that makes it easier for the horse to carry you and for you to give subtle aids, it is important to loosen and soften your hips. The more mature we become, the stiffer we are in the hips, so we must work at this. You don't need the suppleness of a gymnast, but the softer you are in the hips, the easier it will be for you to ride well.

Without stirrups, you may feel the horse's movement underneath you more than you do when riding with stirrups. Relax and just let the horse move you. Don't try to fix and push your hips with his movement. Sit tall with good posture (see page 51), and after a while it will not feel so bad – you might even enjoy it. Feel that your hips and the small of your back are absorbing the horse's movement. And do keep checking that your hips and thighs are not tightening up.

Trotting without stirrups

Once you feel confident about walking without stirrups, you can progress to trying a sitting trot, but just a few strides at first. Hold the neckstrap or front of the saddle, so that you are not tempted to pull on the horse's mouth. There are several ways in which you can do this; your teacher will advise you, depending on your own level of ability and confidence.

You could hold the reins in one hand and the point of contact with the other, or you could loosen the reins but keep hold of them both, with both hands holding the point of contact. Alternatively, you could be asked to let go of them altogether. If so, a knot will be tied in them and you can use your hands just for holding the point of contact.

If this rider had stirrups, the leathers would hang vertically. In trying to get her leg back from the hip, she has made herself stiff.

This rider has taken her stirrup back but pushed her legs too far forward. The stirrup leather is not hanging vertically but is pushed forward.

Your instructor will usually be close at hand and you will trot no more than a few strides. Try to sit up tall and let your horse move you. You may find that your position slips a little, but as soon as you walk re-arrange yourself to correct it. It is much better to do several short trots where you can put yourself back into the correct position than doing a longer trot where your position just keeps on deteriorating.

Benefits of riding without stirrups

If you keep on practicing without stirrups in small amounts, you will soon feel positive benefits. Your balance will improve, your seat will become deeper, and your legs will become longer. Indeed, you will probably be surprised that after only a few minutes' riding without stirrups when you go to take your stirrups back your legs will feel quite short. If this is the case, well done! You have kept your thighs long and hips soft. You may even need to let the stirrups down a hole, depending on how short they feel.

If you or your instructor feel you cannot yet let the stirrups down, be careful not to move back in the saddle to make room for yourself – this puts you behind the horse's center of motion and will be of no benefit.

Making progress

Once you feel confident about riding without stirrups in walk and trot you are well on the way up the horse riding ladder. As your confidence increases, you will be able to ride for longer without stirrups and start to control your horse without any assistance. You will find that you can ride school figures and stay in balance with your horse. As he turns left you will follow

him rather then hoping that you don't wobble and, more by luck than judgment, go with him. When those words "Drop your stirrups" are said, you will not quake; you will get on with it and use the opportunity to improve your position, balance, and feel of what is going on underneath you. You are well on the way!

Rising trot

Years ago, novices used to spend many hours practicing rising trot without stirrups. There is still a use for this, but nowadays it is not very common. To undertake a rising trot without stirrups, you need to hold your thigh up in a shortened position and make the muscles work hard. Nowadays, riders are encouraged to become softer and more relaxed, so the horse can move freely under them.

Although riding without stirrups can boost your confidence and will help you to progress to bigger and better things, most riders will use stirrups when they are out on a hack.

Chapter 6

Tacking up and untacking

As you progress with your riding, you may wish to know more about looking after horses. Equine language is a minefield and can be very confusing for the uninitiated. It is useful to know the names of the parts of the saddle and bridle as well as how to put them on. Part of learning to ride is learning to tack up and untack your horse. Plan to arrive early and tack up before your lesson.

Carrying the saddle and bridle

Undertaking basic stable management tasks will improve your confidence around horses. Ask your instructor to give you some stable management lessons rather than picking up knowledge on an ad hoc basis. Read books about horse care to further enhance your knowledge.

If you carry the saddle and bridle correctly, then everything is less liable to get in a muddle. Put the headpiece of the bridle and the reins over your shoulder and the saddle over your arm with the pommel toward your elbow. If you ever put the saddle down on the ground, always put the pommel toward the floor and bring the girth up so that it rests between the wall and the cantle to prevent it becoming damaged. You can put the saddle over the stable door, but this is not advisable until your horse is tied up. He may well knock the saddle from the door, leaving it with a broken tree and the school with a large bill for repairing it, or even replacing it with a new saddle.

There is a correct way to carry a saddle and bridle. It keeps the tack safe and prevents you from tripping over anything.

Putting on the halter

To put on your horse's halter, go into his stable with the halter and rope. Put the rope around his neck, then put his nose through the noseband of the halter. Lift the strap over the back of his ears and buckle up the halter, so that the noseband is about two fingers' width below the protruding cheek bone. Always fully do up the buckle of the halter, so there is no danger of it coming undone. Check that the horse's mane is comfortable at the poll.

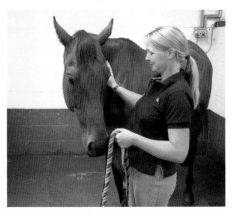

1 Walk up toward your horse's shoulder, talking gently to him and patting him.

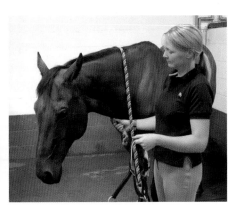

2 Put the rope round his neck. This will give you a basic form of control.

3 Stand facing forward and quickly lift the noseband over the horse's nose.

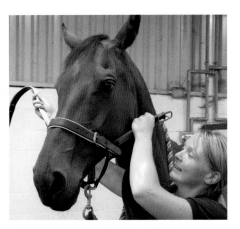

4 While holding up the halter, lift the headpiece over his ears.

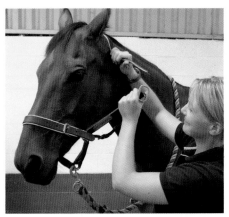

5 Buckle up the halter securely, making sure that it is neither too tight nor too loose.

Types of halter

A leather halter is always safer than a nylon one. If the horse gets caught up on anything, a leather halter will break and release him.

83

Tying up a horse

It is very important that you know how to tie up your horse securely. You will need to do this every time you do something with him, whether he is to be groomed, tacked up, or tied up outside his stable.

To tie up a horse, gently take the rope from round his neck and look for the tie ring on the stable wall. There should be a piece of breakable string attached to the ring and this is what you tie him up to.

It is safer to tie him to a piece of breakable string, so that if he panics for some reason, the string will break and the horse will not damage himself.

Tying a quick-release safety knot
You should always use a quick-release knot, and there are two accepted ways of doing this, as shown below and opposite. Some riding schools prefer using one safety knot to the other, but others do not mind which one you use.

Quick-release knot: method 1

1 Start off by making a loop about halfway down the rope.

2 Now carefully thread the loop through the string attached to the ring on the wall.

3 Make a loop with the loose end of the rope. Pull this through the loop you have made.

4 Now thread the spare end of the rope through the new loop.

Quick-release knot: method 2

1 Start off by putting the loose end of the rope through the string.

2 Make a loop with this piece of rope close to the string.

3 Put this loop across and on top of the other part of the rope.

4 Hold the loose end near the loop; pull it through the loop to make a "U" shape.

5 Now you should pull the rope really taut. Check that it is not loose.

6 Put the loose end through the loop to complete the quick-release knot.

When your horse is tied up, put the saddle on the door where he can't reach it to knock it onto the floor. When tacking up, it does not matter whether you put on the saddle first, or the bridle. Just make sure the horse and tack are safe while you do so. If using a martingale (see page 189), put the bridle on first. You must undo the girth to attach the martingale to it.

The horse's mouth

You may react with horror to the idea of putting your finger in a horse's mouth; the front end bites and the back end kicks! A horse has a gap between his incisor (front) and molar (back) teeth. This is where the bit sits comfortably, and you will not get bitten if you place your finger there. Don't try to put it in the bottom/front of his mouth – that is asking for trouble!

Putting on the bridle

Putting on a bridle can be made to look very easy indeed when it is done by an experienced person. However, it is quite a complicated procedure and one that you must learn to do yourself. If your horse is helpful, it is much easier, but if he decides that he does not want to assist you, it can be very difficult. As you are still learning to tack up, it is essential that a knowledgeable person is present to help and advise you when you are putting on a bridle.

Gaining confidence

If you are confident when you are working around horses, the more they will recognize this and respect you. Having an experienced horse person present will help to boost your confidence and ensure that you undertake the task in a manner to which the horse is accustomed. If you adopt the routine he is used to, he will be more cooperative and relaxed about it all. Always remember that a horse is a creature of habit, and he will be happier with familiar processes that he understands.

Practice makes perfect

It is easy for a horse to lose his confidence and start getting difficult when he is having his bridle put on. Banging the bit on his teeth, inadvertently poking him in the eye or forcing his ears under the headpiece can all lead to a horse becoming worried. However, don't let this put you off trying to put on his bridle. With assistance, you will soon become competent.

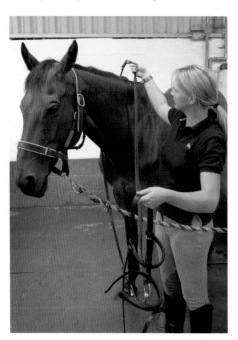

1 Undo the quick-release knot and leave the end slipped through the string. Put the reins over your horse's ears.

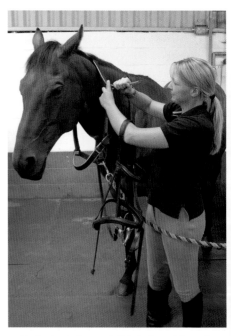

2 Undo the halter and slide it down his neck before doing it up again – by doing so, you will still have control of your horse.

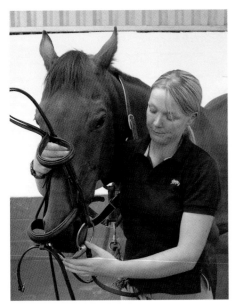

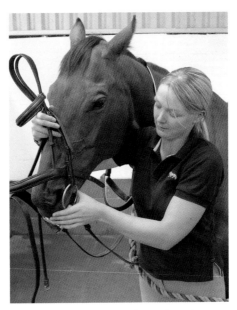

3 Put your right hand under the horse's chin and reach around, so that your hand is in the middle of his face. Hold the bridle at the cheek pieces in your right hand.

4 Bring the bit up toward the teeth and put your left thumb in the side of his mouth at the top of the lips. As he opens his mouth, pull up the bit with your right hand.

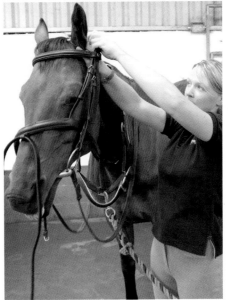

5 Keep pulling the bridle up, and then gently pull the headpiece of the bridle over the horse's right ear.

6 As quickly as you can, put the headpiece over the left ear, so that the bridle is secure on the horse's head.

87

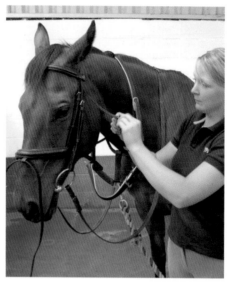

7 Pull the horse's forelock out from under the browband and then make sure that his mane is flat under the headpiece. Now you can do up the throatlatch.

8 You must make sure that the throatlatch is not too tight. You should be able to get a flat hand's width between the horse's cheek bone and the leather.

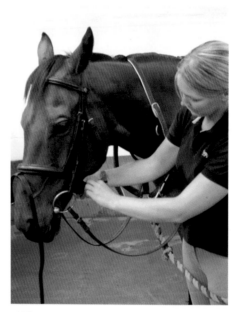

9 The noseband should be done up so that you can get at least one finger between the horse's nose and the leather. Check that the noseband is straight and not lopsided.

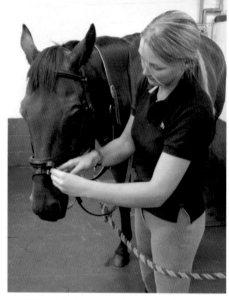

10 This bridle has a noseband that does up under the bit. This helps to keep the horse's mouth shut. The buckle should be away from the mouth.

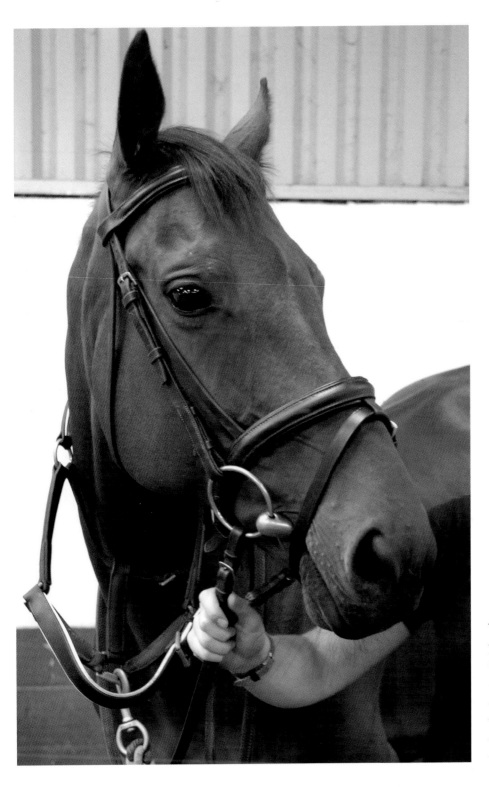

This horse's bridle is fitted correctly. If he is to be tied up, the reins must be twisted and put through the throatlatch. The halter can then be put on over the bridle.

Putting on the saddle

Putting on a saddle is not as complicated as a bridle, but you will still need an expert to assist you the first few times. Make sure that the girth is looped over the seat of the saddle or through the offside stirrup, so it doesn't flap around and hit you or the horse.

Once the saddle is on the horse, check that the saddle pad is still pulled up under the gullet of the saddle and that it is visible all the way around the saddle. A saddle pad pressing on your horse's withers or a saddle that pushes on its outer border can cause pressure points on your horse's back. Different saddle pads can be attached to saddles in a variety of ways. Some, like the one shown here, may have no points of attachment at all, but you should always attach them if there are fittings to do so – this will help to stop the saddle pad sliding back under the saddle.

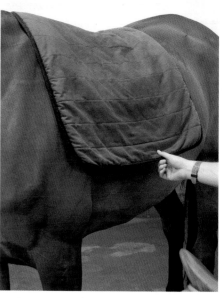

1 Always put the saddle pad on a little further forward than the position in which you finally want the saddle to be. Do make sure that it is equal on both sides of the horse.

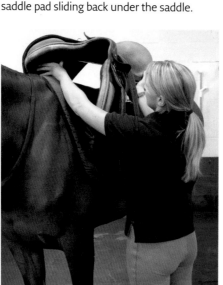

2 Take the saddle in both hands and lift it up so that you place it on top of the saddle pad. Again, it should be a little further forward than the final position (as shown opposite in picture 7).

3 Pull the saddle pad up into the saddle's gullet. With the heel of your palm, push the pommel down and back until the saddle stops at the point where it sits correctly on the horse's back.

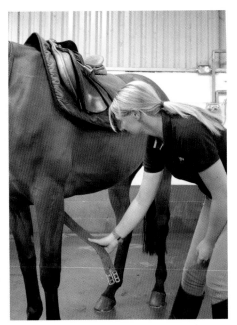

4 Go around to the offside of the horse and pull down the girth. Now go back around to the horse's nearside and bring the girth around under the belly and up toward the saddle.

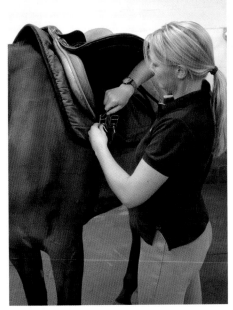

5 Buckle the girth up on the first and third straps. Only do the girth up tight enough that it will not slip around the horse's belly or too far back, and it will make the saddle secure.

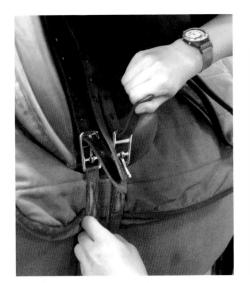

6 Frequently, you may find that as you do up the girth the saddle pad will crease up. If so, it must be flattened out so that it does not cause a pressure point on the horse's back.

7 You can see here that the girth lies in the correct position just behind the horse's elbow. The saddle pad has been straightened out and is still pulled up under the gullet of the saddle.

Untacking tips

If you have a very big horse, then it may be worth going around to the off side and putting the girth on to the seat of the saddle before lifting it off. Have a glance to make sure that the saddle has not rubbed him, and then give him a quick rub with your hand to help the circulation.

Taking off the saddle

To untack a horse it is probably better to take the saddle off first, but, again, there is no hard and fast rule. Make sure you have the halter at hand – if you are unsure, you might want to tie up the horse first. After you've taken off the saddle, it may be necessary to brush or wash any rub marks. Tell the staff if you notice any of these.

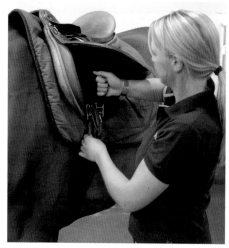

1 To take off the saddle, lift up the saddle flap and then undo both girth buckles.

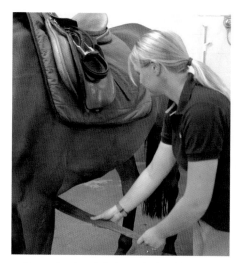

2 Do not let the girth drop; the buckles may hit your horse's leg. Put the girth down carefully.

3 Slide the saddle and saddle pad back and lift them up from your horse's back with both hands. As you lift, put them over one arm.

4 Reach for the girth with the other arm and put it over the saddle. Now you can put the saddle down somewhere safe.

Taking off the bridle

When you take off a bridle, it is essential that you are very careful not to catch your horse's teeth with the bit. As with all things when dealing with horses, you need to be confident and efficient. Be patient as you take the bridle over your horse's ears. Let it down slowly over his face and wait for him to open his mouth to allow the bit to come out. If you are in a hurry and do this too quickly, you may knock his teeth, and the next time you do it he may react anxiously and throw his head up.

A little patience on your part can help to prevent a bad habit forming in the future. Remember to praise your horse and give him a pat to reward him for letting you ride him and for being patient.

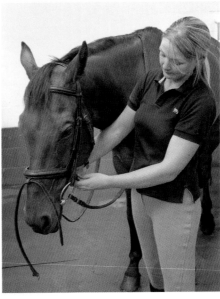

1 To take off the horse's bridle, you should start by undoing the noseband together with the flash noseband strap if there is one.

Practice makes perfect

When you start to tack up your horse, you may feel that it is nearly impossible, but when you have done it a few times you will know where to position yourself and will start to anticipate what the horse is going to do and thus be one step ahead of him. You will soon become efficient and wonder why you ever thought the job difficult.

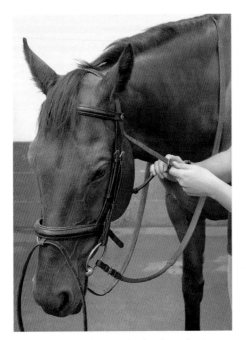

2 Your next task is to undo the throatlatch. Having done this, you can bring the reins up to the horse's poll.

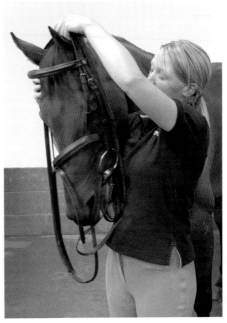

3 Stand facing forward and put your right hand under the horse's jaw. Reach for the headpiece and gently lift it over his ears.

Changing sides

It is a good idea to change sides for the stirrup leathers each time you strip clean the saddle. The leather on the near side tends to stretch more because it is used for mounting, so if you change them around they should stretch equally.

Putting a snaffle bridle together

1 Take the browband and then fold it the way in which it sits on the horse.

2 Slide it through the headpiece, so it is forward of the throatlatch on the right.

3 If possible, hang the bridle from a hook, and then attach the cheek pieces.

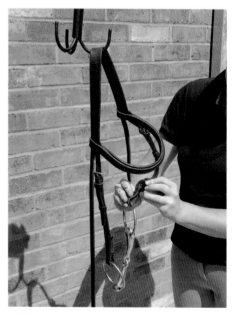

4 Make sure the bit is the correct way around and then attach it to the cheek pieces.

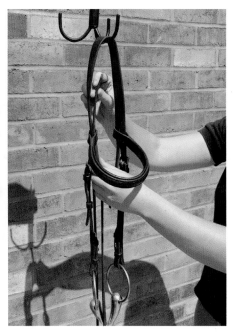

5 Now thread the noseband through the inside of the browband and headpiece.

6 Take the noseband up under the headpiece and down through the near side of the browband.

7 Do up the noseband on the left-hand side (nearside) of the bridle.

8 Attach the reins to the back of the bit. Buckle fittings on reins face outward; bits inward.

Chapter 7

Refining your riding skills

How do you feel about your riding lessons? Are you looking forward to the next one? Does each lesson seem too short? Are you feeling confident about the skills that you have acquired so far? If the answer to all these questions is "yes," then it sounds as if you are making good progress and enjoying your riding. However, if your answers are "no," you need to sit down and think very carefully about your equestrian future.

Making riding more enjoyable

If you are still keen to ride but do not feel happy about what you are doing, maybe your riding school is not the one for you. Discuss your feelings with your teachers and see if they come up with any suggestions. If they are unable to help, then consider trying another school. It could be the change you need to move you forward.

If you are still feeling nervous, discuss this with your instructor, too. Some novice riders are anxious because they do not feel secure on the horse. However, if you work hard on improving your position, this will help you to move forward; it is not pleasant to feel unsafe and out of control.

Work within your limits

Do not be worried about discussing your feelings – a good instructor will understand and help you. It is vital not to let anybody convince you to progress faster than you feel is within your limits, as this is where the problems and doubts can occur. Like all other sports, there is a major psychological element within riding and you must feel content mentally and physically.

Learning to canter

This principle holds strongly when you start to learn to canter. If you do not feel ready, then do not let anybody convince you to "have a go." Confidence is vital for success in learning this skill. As in all other aspects of learning to ride, it is essential to have a horse who knows his job and will help you to learn. Mentally, cantering is a big step up and you have enough to think about

without having the "wrong tools for the job." Even when you are ready to learn to canter, you may still feel apprehensive, although if you are well prepared, this will be outweighed by your desire to try.

Making the transition

When a horse makes a transition to canter, he moves from the two-beat pace of the trot to a three-beat pace. Consequently, the movement created by the horse is completely different to that of the trot. There are two ways in which a horse can make the sequence of three beats, and when he is in a ménage he should always be cantering with the "leading leg" being the same as the rein he is on. This sounds rather complicated, but if your horse is experienced he will be balanced enough to strike off with the correct leading leg for you.

Beat numbers one, two and three

To canter in a ménage, the first leg the horse puts down is the outside hind leg. An easy way to remember beat number two is to think: "Beat number two is two legs together." This is the diagonal pair of legs – inside hind and outside fore.

The third beat is created by the only other leg yet to be put down – the inside front leg. This beat number three is also called the leading leg and looks as if it is leading your horse forward because it comes furthest forward.

Suspension

After beat number three, there is always a moment of suspension when all four legs are off the ground together, and then the outside hind leg starts the sequence again.

1 The horse's outside hind leg is the first one to be put down and starts the right lead canter.

2 The diagonal pair of legs, inside hind and outside fore, come forward and down together to make beat number two.

3 The inside fore leg is the last leg to be put down by the horse to create beat number three. This is called the leading leg. It should be the inside front leg when in a ménage (riding ring).

4 The horse is just about to take its weight from the inside fore leg to create a brief moment of suspension before the inside hind leg steps under to start the sequence again.

Chapter 8

Hacking out

When you feel confident about cantering and can maintain good balance with your horse, you are ready to take a major step forward. What most riders look forward to is hacking out. This can be really good fun, relaxing, and exhilarating, but it may be something you feel apprehensive about. Do not worry if you have that sinking feeling about hacking out. Just as when you learned to canter, do not let people push you into something you don't feel ready for. Only you will know when the time comes to try hacking out.

Your first hack

The first time you hack out, your riding school may decide that just you and your instructor will go out together. This is less daunting than going out with a group, but it may not be possible, depending on how busy the riding school is. If you feel that you are ready to go out for a hack, discuss this with your instructor first. They will know the area and the hacks that are available.

This horse and rider are easily visible to other road users. Notice the two fetlock bands, positioned on the outside legs.

Keep it simple

Your first hack should be as uncomplicated as possible, with easy terrain and routes that are relatively enclosed. It is always best to hack out on a horse that you have already ridden. This will help to boost your confidence as you will know and trust him.

However much you are looking forward to escaping from the confines of the riding school, a one-hour hack is probably long enough for your first venture into the outside world, as this is the length of time that you would normally ride in a lesson.

Clothing

Make sure you dress for the weather. For example, if it is raining, then make sure you have a waterproof jacket – there is nothing more miserable then getting soaking wet. If the weather is fine and sunny, do not be tempted to wear a sleeveless or strappy top. It is always advisable to ride with your arms covered, even when it is hot, so that if you should be unfortunate enough to fall off, your arms will be protected and you will not damage the skin. Otherwise you are advised to wear normal riding wear (see page 24).

High-visibility clothing
If you have to go out on to the road, it is strongly recommended that you and your horse wear high-visibility gear. Reflective bands around your horse's fetlocks are extremely effective as drivers tend to look down toward the curb when they are driving. A tabard and light-colored gloves for yourself are useful and will help to attract other road users' attention.

Where to ride

Hacking out is great fun and a good way to see the countryside. Beaches and open spaces are many riders' idea of perfection. Fresh air, good company, and a horse are a recipe for riding happiness.

This rider is wearing light-colored gloves, so that other road users will be able to see her hand signals more easily. If you carry a whip when riding on the road, hold it in your left hand to help keep your horse to the right side of the road, facing traffic.

113

Don't overtake

A rule that most riding schools will apply is that you should never overtake the rider in front of you when you are hacking out. This can cause the horses to become overexcited and you may well soon be going faster than any of you want to!

Hacking guidelines

Before you start your hack, your instructor will run through a few rules. For health and safety reasons, do your best to observe them. Different riding schools have different regulations, depending on the number of people on the hack and the terrain you are going over. If there are three or four of you going out, there will probably be an assistant for your instructor who will ride at the rear. They will be able to keep a careful eye on what is going on and will be able to assist you if there are any problems.

Mounting up

You will probably mount up in the stable yard and be put in a riding order that suits the horses. Make sure your girth is tight and your stirrups feel comfortable. If you have developed a fairly long length of stirrup for riding in the school, you may well be advised to shorten your stirrups a little. Your instructor will be able to advise you about the length of your stirrups.

Two abreast or single file?

Your teacher will let you know which way to ride. Sometimes riding two abreast is suitable, while at other times you will be in single file. If you have to go on the road, try and keep well to the right-hand side. If you carry a whip, make sure it is in your left hand; this will help keep your horse to the right.

If you're going to hack out regularly, read about or ask your instructor to review trail riding safety for you. One important rule is to never ride out alone. Also, always let someone at the barn know where you're going and approximately what time to expect you back. Carry a cell phone with you in case you need to call for help. Pack a hoof pick, in case your horse picks up a stone in his shoe. A halter and a lead rope may be handy for longer rides, if you plan to take rest breaks. Always wear your safety helmet. An upper body protective vest is also good to wear in the field, to protect your back and torso during falls on hard or rocky ground.

These riders have mounted in the yard and are going out on a hack that does not involve road work. Some riding schools, but not all, may insist that you have your arms completely covered.

These riders are lucky
enough to be able to
ride over fields and
tracks. They are riding
in single file and are
keeping a sensible
distance apart. They
are not too close to the
horse in front to get
kicked, but not so far
away that their horses
may become worried
about being left behind.

This horse and rider are enjoying an exhilarating canter up a hill. For many people, there is no better way to relax and enjoy their riding than to go out into the countryside for a hack.

Cantering

If you are enjoying your first hack out and are feeling secure and confident, you may be given an opportunity to have your first canter outside. This will give you a real sense of achievement and may well feel easier than when you do it in the school because you will be traveling in a straight line and your horse will find it easier to balance himself.

Be prepared and alert

When you are out hacking, you must always be prepared for the unexpected.

Do not be tempted to ride along on a loose rein, totally absorbed in gossip with other riders – there is always the possibility of something spooking your horse. Even the most unflappable horse can be frightened by a stray plastic carrier bag being blown toward you or by a pheasant flying up from behind a hedge.

Remember that horses are creatures of flight – in the wild, if they are frightened by anything, they would rather run than stay and fight. They will only fight if they are cornered. However, if you can successfully negotiate hazards, it will help to increase your confidence and improve your balance, thus making you a better rider.

Improving your balance

Riding out over hills and rough terrain will help to improve your balance. If you are going up a steep hill, incline your body slightly forward, keeping the weight into your heels. This will help the horse to get up the hill and be great for your balance. If you feel you are unable to keep your weight forward, hold a piece of mane or the neckstrap to help you.

When riding downhill, do not lean too far back. Keep your weight in to your heels and think of sitting upright. The steeper the downhill gradient, the more you need to think of "leaning back."

When riding downhill, it is sensible to walk to help you and your horse keep your balance. As you become increasingly proficient as a rider, you can try it in trot and then in canter.

These riders are riding two abreast. The horses are used to this and are behaving well. They do not think that it is a race, and they are not nervous of each other. They are swinging along in a forward trot.

117

Chapter 9

Learning to jump

Just when you are starting to feel confident about your riding, your instructor will throw something else in to test you. How about learning to jump? You may have similar anxieties to the ones you had when you were learning to canter, or going out on your first hack. Remember those feelings and how you overcame them – you can do the same with jumping. Every rider should learn at least the basics of jumping. Many horses love to jump, and you will discover that it really is fun.

The right horse

Initially, when your teacher broaches the subject of learning to jump, you may well feel that jumping is not something you really want to do, but it is always useful to have at least a basic knowledge of jumping, so that if you come across a log or a ditch when you are out hacking you have the ability to get to the other side.

Do not let anyone push you into learning to jump, but do be prepared to have a go. Many people feel that jumping is one step too far for them, but an all-around horse person should be able to jump even if it is only very small obstacles.

It is vital that you are taught to jump on a reliable horse. Your favorite might not enjoy jumping, so you may have to use another horse. There are two main reasons why many people do not enjoy jumping, and these are outlined below.

The first is that they are taught on horses who are not reliable over a fence and are therefore unsure as to how they will get to the other side safely. The other reason is that they are not taught correctly and that their position is insecure. When a horse jumps, he transfers his weight to his hindquarters, pushes down to give himself spring, stretches out over the jump, lands on his front feet, and then brings his hind legs under him.

Consequently, you, the rider, need to be able to follow this movement, and to make this easier for yourself, you may need to shorten your stirrups. The number of holes depends on several factors. Your instructor will help you get the correct length.

This rider has a secure position for jumping. Her weight is pushed down the back of her leg into her heel to give a strong lower leg.

This rider is shortening her stirrups ready for jumping. She is doing this incorrectly as she has taken her feet out of the stirrups.

120

Jumping positions

Before you start to jump, it is important to become secure in the "light seat" position. Within the horse world, there are several names for this position – some people call it the forward seat, others the poised position, but whatever name you use, they are all the same thing. There is also a great deal of discussion as to whether these are all the same as the "jumping position." This is not something for us to get bogged down with here, but you should discuss all this with your riding instructor, so that you are both talking about the same thing.

Forward position

The jumping position is seen as a more forward position that is taken when going over a fence, whereas the light seat is viewed as being halfway between this and the flatwork position. There are many variations of the light seat, and as long as the rider remains in balance with the horse, then some people may well have to be more forward than others.

Notice how this rider's stirrups are a little too long, and thus he is trying to stand in the stirrups rather than fold.

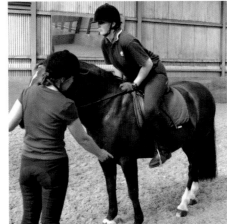

This rider is not pushing her weight down into her heels. She is insecure and rests her hand on her horse's neck for balance.

This rider has allowed her lower leg to slip back too far, and, consequently, she has collapsed on to her horse's neck.

This rider is becoming more insecure as his lower leg slips further back. He needs to work to keep his weight into his heels.

A light seat

As you will discover, the most important part of your light seat is your lower leg. This is actually your anchor, and if it stays underneath you, supporting your body weight, then you will be very secure when you are jumping. If your lower leg comes back, you will tip forward; and if it is pushed too far forward, your body weight will be pushed back behind your horse's point of balance.

Shorten your reins

You should shorten your reins in the light seat position because your hands need to

1 This rider is practicing the light seat in the canter, and is working on undulating ground.

2 Notice how she is completely in balance with her horse, with a secure lower leg.

3 Here the horse and rider are both focused on what they are doing and are looking forward.

4 On the third beat of left canter, the rider still has a secure lower leg, although her knee is just a little tight.

These riders have all shortened their stirrups and are about to practice their light seat work.

move forward a little along the line of the reins towards your horse's mouth. Do not reach so far forward with your arms that you push yourself out of balance, but if your hands are a little forward either side of your horse's neck, they will follow the stretch of his neck and not interfere with his motion. Nothing puts a horse off jumping quicker than being pulled and restricted in his mouth.

Take it gradually

As a novice rider, you must be secure in your light seat in all paces before moving on to pole work and jumping. This is not something to be rushed; it has to be

worked for and practiced. You will probably feel some pulling in the tendons and the ligaments down the back of your legs initially when you start working on your light seat. Ask your instructor if you can rest your legs by taking them out of the stirrups for a minute or two at halt – this will help to relax your legs.

Your upper body

Your back should not collapse and become rounded as you incline forward a little from the hips. As has been discussed earlier, the amount that you incline your upper body forward can differ for different body

To stretch out the back of your legs, stand with the balls of your feet on the edge of a bottom step and then push down on your heels.

shapes, and as long as you are secure and remain in balance that is all that matters. You should look between your horse's ears, and don't forget to smile!

Practice in halt

You need to practice this position in the halt until you can find your balance easily and feel secure. You may well feel a stretch down the back of your legs. An exercise you can do to help this is to stand on the balls of your feet on a step or the bottom stair and push down on to your heels. Do this a few times, then rest and repeat. A simple exercise of touching your toes will help to stretch the back of your legs.

Practice at walk

When you are happy that you are able to maintain your light seat in halt, you can move on to trying it at walk. As soon as the horse moves, you may have to readjust your balance to stay with your horse. Do not pull on the reins to balance yourself.

If you have a neckstrap, it should be a high one, which is positioned around your horse's neck where your hands should be. If you do not have a neckstrap, hold the mane, although this does encourage you to put your hands up the horse's neck rather than following the line of the reins. Do not hold this position for long periods, as you can quite easily strain yourself.

Practice the trot and canter

Once you can balance yourself in walk, it is time to try the trot. In this position,

it is better not to do rising trot, but to hover a little above the saddle. Make sure that your weight stays down into your heels, and your knees and hips stay soft, so you can absorb the movement. If you thought the walk was difficult, then the trot will be even more so! Again, it only takes practice in small amounts to build up your feel and body fitness.

Needless to say, once you have managed the trot, you are ready to move on to the canter. Try to give your aids for canter in the light seat, rather than sitting down and then taking the position again. By the time you are efficient in the trot, you will not find the canter too onerous, although giving the aids in light seat is quite difficult. It is hard work but worth it for the security you will achieve in your jumping.

Practice over trotting poles

The next step is to practice your light seat over trotting poles. You instructor will probably put out a single pole first for you to get the feel of it. Your horse may lift his legs a little higher as he goes over them.

This gives you more movement to absorb and helps you stay in balance. It is accepted practice that if the trotting poles are placed in such a way that there is not a stride between them, you go from one pole to three. This is so your horse does not get confused and think he has to jump them. You will practice going over single poles and lines of poles in various parts of the school. Some may be on the long side and others across the diagonal, which helps to improve your balance. Going around corners and turns in the light seat is the next step.

This rider is riding over a single pole in the light seat. Her upper body is balanced, but her reins could be a little shorter with the hands toward the horse's mouth.

Notice how this rider has lost his balance as his lower leg slips back. His reins are in loops as he has had to rest his hands on his horse's neck to balance himself.

This rider is trying very hard to make sure that everything is correct. Consequently, she is very tight and tense. She just needs to relax more and keep on practicing.

This rider is working in balance over three trotting poles. The horse looks happy in his work, which is always a sign that both the rider and horse are working together in harmony.

Preparing to jump

By now you should be very secure and the weight should stay down in to your heels without you particularly having to think about it. At this stage, you are ready to move on to actually jumping! It may all seem a rather long and slow build up, but by doing it this way you are ensuring that you are safe. Time spent practicing your light seat will never be wasted!

Your first jump

This will normally be a cross pole with a placing pole in front of it to ensure that your horse reaches the jump at the correct point for take off. A cross pole jump is inviting for both you and the horse and encourages you to jump in the middle.

Your first jump may well be from trot. It needs to be active, but not running. However, if you can feel and create the pace for your horse to go over the trotting poles actively, then that is the approach pace you need for the jump.

Take up your trot and light seat and make a good approach turn, so you are heading for the middle of the fence. Stay in your light seat, and take hold of the neckstrap or mane and keep your legs on. Your horse should help you out by keeping the same rhythm over the placing pole and then over the fence. Try to keep breathing with your weight in your heels, and do allow yourself to collapse as your horse lands on the other side.

Your horse may well only treat the jump as a high trotting pole, but do not worry if this is the case as it will give you a chance to get to the other side of a jump without making too much effort. Congratulate yourself that you have done it – and safely, too. Once you have done this a few times, you can start to breathe as you go over the fence and also begin to think a little more about what is going on.

This horse and rider have approached the middle of the cross pole and are jumping it in good form. They are both looking forward and are jumping straight over the middle of the jump.

1 This horse and rider are approaching the placing pole in trot. The trot could be a little more forward.

2 The horse is going over the placing pole. The rider should have adopted a light seat by now in order to stay in balance.

3 The horse takes off over the cross pole. The rider is holding the neckstrap, so as not to interfere with the horse's mouth.

4 The horse lands after the fence and helps the rider by continuing forward in a straight line.

5 The horse and rider have taken the placing pole in canter, but the rider is not disturbed by this.

6 They are still in harmony as the horse jumps the cross pole from canter. He should only do this if he is asked to canter.

Five phases

A horse's jump always consists of the following five phases: the approach; the take off; flight; the landing; and getaway. The getaway can also be the approach to the next fence if you are jumping more than one obstacle. The horse should be obedient and in balance through all phases of the jump. A person learning to jump should never be asked to ride a horse who is not established in his jumping, or doubt can enter the rider's mind. A novice jumping horse and a novice rider do not go together.

1 This horse and rider are approaching a fence in canter. She is in balance with a light contact on the reins.

2 Here the horse is arriving at the fence and is preparing to take off and jump it.

3 The horse is undertaking the second phase of the jump: the take off. The rider's lower leg should be a little more secure.

4 This is the third phase of the jump: the flight over the fence. Both the horse and rider are looking forward.

5 The fourth phase of the jump is the landing. The rider's lower leg is very secure here. Some riders, especially novice ones, tend to collapse when the horse lands.

6 Here you can see the fifth and final phase of the jump – the getaway. Although this horse and rider are not approaching another fence, they could do so if they wished.

This horse and rider are jumping the middle of the fence. The rider is in balance with the horse, and they are looking forward. The rider's position is secure, and they both appear to be enjoying themselves.

129

Watch others jumping

Jumping is not an easy skill to learn. The problem is that three of the five phases of the jump - the take off, flight, and landing - all happen very quickly and are not always the same. When you are learning to jump, and even when you are more proficient, these problems can make practicing the skill difficult. If you watch people jumping, this will help you to progress. Do not worry if you cannot achieve a perfect position and maintain total balance with your horse every time he jumps. The most important thing is not to use your reins to help you to balance - this is the job of your lower leg. As you become more proficient, you will stay in balance with your horse more easily, and as your feel and confidence improve you will really start to enjoy your jumping.

1 Here you can see that the rider is making a good approach to the fence in balance.

2 The rider tries to take off before the horse, but her balance is too far forward, making it difficult for the horse to take off.

3 Because the rider's lower leg is secure, she is able to take the fence safely and land without too many problems.

4 The rider is approaching the fence again, but this time she remains in balance at take off.

Over the flight of this fence, the rider's lower leg is insecure, so she has to rest her hands on the neck to balance herself.

On take off at this fence, notice how the rider has lost the rein contact, and her lower leg could be a little more secure.

This rider has lost rein contact but she is in balance and riding positively forward. Both horse and rider look happy and secure.

As this rider takes off, she is pushing her upper body too far forward over her hands, so her elbows are sticking out.

Practice

Jumping is all about practice. When you are learning to jump, it may be advisable to have two half-hour lessons a week rather than a single one-hour lesson. Like any sport and practical skill, the more you can practice the better you will become.

Perfecting your jumping

Once you are happy about going over a fence, your job as the rider is to get your horse to the fence in rhythm and balance. His job is to get you safely to the other side.

Landing in canter

When you feel competent jumping a fence from trot, try to approach the fence a little more positively. Aim to try and land in canter and then canter away from the jump. If you are riding in a ménage, your coach may well put a second fence on the other side of the school, so that you land in canter, canter around the short side of the arena, maintain the rhythm and positive feel to the canter, and then you approach the second fence. You have now jumped two linked fences together and have also jumped from canter – a major step forward.

It sometimes feels easier to jump from canter, but as people progress they often start to get worried about "seeing a stride" to a fence and they forget to ride forward. Do not worry about trying to see a stride; instead, just put all your efforts in to maintaining a good canter. If the quality of the canter is good – purposeful and balanced, taking you forward but not rushing – your horse will arrive at the fence correctly. It is only when you start to jump over approximately 3 feet (1 m) high that you need to think about "seeing a stride."

Circle before you start to jump

You should try to get into the habit of cantering at least one circle before you approach a jump, so that you feel the canter is positive. Of course, you cannot do this for every fence if you are linking some together in a course, but part of the skill of jumping a course is to be able to maintain the quality of the canter, especially when you are going around corners.

One stride double

When you can link two or three fences together spaced out around the ménage, and you are able to maintain your balance, guide your horse accurately and help him to maintain his rhythm, the time has come to start thinking about jumping fences closer together.

There are various types of closely linked fences – a double, a bounce, and a related distance. These fences can also be linked together to form gridwork.

The easiest type of linked fences to jump is a one stride double. This is where your horse jumps one fence, takes one stride of canter, then jumps a second. Your teacher will probably get you to jump the first fence a few times and then put the second one in for you. You may be asked to approach the first fence in trot and then land in canter, or you may approach in canter. It will depend on your horse and your level of competence. Your teacher may then put a third fence in for you to jump in a line.

Boost your confidence

Although jumping fences closer together may seem daunting, if your horse helps you, then you can perfect your fold over the fence and feel your security improve. If all is going well, your confidence will increase, you will feel more relaxed, and jumping will be challenging and fun.

1 This horse and rider are approaching the first element of a one stride double fence.

2 Notice how both the horse and rider are focusing on the middle of the fence and are committed to the jump.

3 As they prepare for the take off, the rider just gets in front of the horse's balance and realizes her mistake.

4 Balance is regained, but the horse takes off a little right of center as his weight has gone through his right shoulder.

5 The horse and rider are now focused on the second jump. The rider's lower leg has slipped back a little.

6 As they land, they are both looking at the second fence and are committed to going forward.

7 The horse brings his hind legs to the ground and the rider stays in balance.

8 The horse now takes a stride of canter. Notice that the rider is maintaining good rein control and security.

9 The horse takes off at the second fence. This time he is positioned at the middle of the fence.

10 The rider's balance is a little forward but not so much that it is interfering with the quality of the horse's jump

11 As they land, the rider shows a very good lower leg and balance. Her upper body is a little round.

12 The get away from the second element of the double shows they could move to another fence if necessary.

Gridwork

There are many different combinations of fences that can be used to vary the number of strides between fences and the number jumped. Gridwork is fantastic for your jumping position, balance, and suppleness. The fences are set up so that everything happens easily, and the horse will take you through the grid once you are in.

Benefits of gridwork

The fold through your hips will improve as will your feel and the way you follow your horse's movement. Your lower leg will become more secure and your hands and arms will follow the stretch of the horse's head. Gridwork is hard work for your horse, so you'll have to be content with only going down the grid a few times each lesson.

Jumping a bounce

When your instructor tells you that they are going to put up a bounce for you, either as part of a grid or by itself, then you should feel very proud of yourself. A bounce is where your horse jumps a fence, lands, and then takes off again for the second fence.

This exercise is extremely hard work for your horse, and, as such, he will put a great deal of energy into jumping this exercise. Consequently, he will move you, the rider, more than he will for a double or for a series of fences making a course. However, as long as your lower leg is secure, you will be able to absorb the movement and go with it. If you can achieve this, you can feel very pleased indeed as you are now well on your way to becoming an extremely competent jumper.

1 This horse and rider are approaching a three-jump grid. The first jump is a cross pole to encourage straightness and to make it more inviting.

2 The horse has landed and is looking at the next fence. This gives the rider a positive feeling of going forward. The horse knows his job and is focused on the next fence.

3 The horse brings his hind legs underneath him and then moves forward into the one non-jumping stride. He is still helping the rider by thinking forward.

4 The horse takes the non-jumping stride. The rider must be careful to follow the horse's movement and not to anticipate the next jump.

5 Here the horse is preparing to take off for the second fence. This is a simple inviting upright fence. The rider is anticipating the take off a little too much.

6 The horse takes off. The rider needs to ensure that her lower leg stays secure under her body. She is becoming a little tense; her face gives this away.

137

7 The horse lands and shows that he is not necessarily focusing yet on the next fence. The rider's leg is secure and is keeping her position safe.

8 The horse has now seen the third fence as his hind legs come under him. Notice how the rider is in very good balance with the horse.

9 The horse takes the one non-jumping stride again. Note that the rider is just a little in front of the horse and needs to correct her position. Her hands are helping her balance.

10 The horse is now preparing to take off at the third fence, which is a simple spread fence. The rider's balance has been regained and is good.

11 The horse takes off over the fence. The rider has exaggerated her fold. This may be due to the fact that this fence is a spread. Consequently, her hands are resting on the horse's neck.

12 The horse is stretched out over the spread fence. Both the horse and rider are positive. The rider has regained her balance and she is very secure.

13 The horse and rider land safely after the third element and have performed well through the grid. The rider is showing empathy and has not disrupted her horse's ability to perform.

14 The getaway shows that both are thinking positively and enjoying themselves. Occasional loss of balance through the grid has not been so great as to be detrimental to the horse.

Chapter 10

What if something goes wrong?

As with any other sport, when you are learning to ride things can sometimes go wrong. Riding is a sport where you have another living, thinking being that you have to take into consideration – your horse – and this is one of the reasons why you may have the odd bad day. Remember that all riders, no matter how experienced, will encounter problems that they need to overcome.

Earn your horse's respect

Your horse may not always be on the same wavelength as you. He may come out of his stable one day and feel a little off color; or he may come in from the field having been pestered by flies for hours and thus be tired and miserable. The list is almost endless. This is why, as a novice rider, it is useful to ride the same horse as often as possible. By doing so, you can start to build up a relationship with him and get to know his moods.

Well-schooled horses

The better schooled your horse is, the less he will let his moods affect his way of going, but, just like a moody teenager, there may well be days when you seem to be unable to get the horse on your side. As you progress with your riding ability and your confidence grows, these days will become fewer as your horse will respect you more and will not feel that he is able to ignore you.

A good riding school will keep the horses that novice riders use "tuned up," with the staff schooling them regularly, hacking them out and possibly even taking them to competitions. This will help them to stay generous and to assist you rather than ignore you. Although it is better to ride the same horse until you feel confident, if you feel that your horse is starting to take advantage of you,

Here the rider is riding past the rear of the ride. This may sound like an easy exercise, but with the horse's herd instincts, he will want to go to his friends rather than past them.

discuss this with your coach and see if you can try another horse.

One reason why your horse may be ignoring you is that you are being asked to undertake tasks on him that you are not yet capable of achieving. For example, you may be asked in a group lesson to ride your horses past the rear of the ride. Your horse may decide that he is going to stay with his friends and, if this is the case, you will be unable to make him do what you want.

Good relations

It is important to build a relationship with the horse you are riding. If you do not gel with the horse, ask your teacher if you can try another one. Just as with people, there will be some horses you do not get on with.

This horse and rider are tuned in to each other. Their mutual trust is such that they can tackle a grid of fences and appear at ease.

143

Stiffness

If you have difficulties trying to work toward a correct, in-balance position, it may be due to stiffness. Indeed, many people turn to other forms of exercise in an effort to increase their suppleness and flexibility. Yoga, T'ai Chi and The Alexander Technique have all proved useful for riders with stiffness problems. One of them may suit you – you can only try.

Lunge lessons

If your riding aids are not sufficiently well coordinated or strong enough to undertake an exercise like passing the rear of the ride, you will have to work on improving your position and core stability. The best thing to help with this is to have some lunge

This rider is having a lunge lesson on a well-mannered horse who is used to this type of work. This helps her to concentrate on her position while the coach controls the horse.

lessons, so that you do not have to worry about controlling your horse and you can concentrate on your position.

You can work on your depth of seat to improve your core stability and security. As a result of this, you will find that if you ask your horse to do something and he disagrees, then your position will not be compromised. You will be able to maintain enough balance and strength of position to be able to tell him quite positively that you want him to obey you.

Using a crop

Once you have an independent seat and do not use your hands to help yourself balance, your teacher may suggest that you ride with a crop or whip to help back up your aids. When you have mastered the art of carrying and using a crop, a horse who is prone to ignoring your leg usually becomes more responsive and respectful of your aids. Riding school horses, especially,

tend to know when you are carrying a whip and can be transformed into paragons of obedience. However, some horses will not tolerate you carrying a whip; these are usually the more sensitive ones.

Many people feel that a whip is cruel, and in the wrong hands it can be. Whips tend to be used to remind a horse that he has to listen to your leg. Consequently, when you give your horse a leg aid, you first give him

The side reins on the horse help keep control and encourage him forward into the bridle.

145

When you are carrying any whip, be it long or short, it should go through your hand and rest across the middle of your thigh. Do not rest your thumb on the whip; this will stiffen your hand.

the opportunity to respond. If he does not react, the second time you use your leg, do it in conjunction with your whip. Use the whip as close to your leg as possible, so he connects the two. Hopefully, the next time you use your leg, he will respond to it immediately without the use of the whip.

Types of whips

There are two kinds of whips you can carry: a short whip (crop), which is used for jumping and hacking out, and a dressage whip, which is longer and is used for flatwork. The short whip is easier to hold and control but is more difficult to use correctly.

Using a short whip

When you are riding in a ménage, usually you should carry your whip in your inside hand to ensure that your horse is listening to your inside leg. This is the dominant leg, telling him to go forward by motivating his inside hind leg.

To use a short whip, you need to put both your reins into the hand that is not holding the whip. This is so you can move your hand back to use it behind your leg. If you don't do this, you will be pulling your horse in his mouth as you use the whip. You would then be telling him to stop and go at the same time – a recipe for confusion.

Changing the whip over

When you change the short whip over when changing the rein, it does not matter where you do it. Just choose a convenient place that will not upset your horse's balance or way of going. This may be after the corner when you have changed the rein. Some people maintain that you must change the whip as you go across the diagonal, but this is not the case.

Again, it is only practice that will make you efficient at changing the whip over. At first, you will be a little clumsy, but do not give up. You will find that you are more comfortable holding the whip in one particular hand. You need to ensure that you are happy carrying the stick in both hands, but, again, this will come with practice and experience.

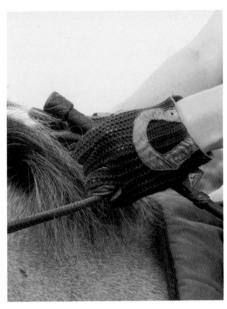

The whip should always be held through your hand and positioned between your thumb and the first finger.

Types of whip

There are many different makes and styles of whip. If you are going to purchase one, discuss with your teacher which length will be best for you and the horses you ride. Always buy a whip that has a weight and balance that suits you.

1 To change the whip, put both the reins into the hand that is holding the whip.

2 Pull the whip through over the horse's withers and in front of your body.

Long whips

A long whip tends to be used only when you are riding in a ménage. You are not allowed to compete in jumping competitions with a long whip. If you are planning to compete one day, you will have to learn how to use both types of whip.

Using a dressage whip

To use a long whip, all you need to do is learn how to flick your wrist and hand in a quick sideways movement. Your hand stays still, so there is no necessity to put your reins in to the other hand. Think of turning your little finger in and up a little in a short, sharp movement. This will move your hand and forearm and make the end of the whip flick on to the horse behind your leg. Initially, you may find that you catch yourself with the whip, but don't worry – you will soon learn the technique.

Changing over a dressage whip

This is different from using a short whip. The whip is too long to bring through in front of you, so you will need to learn the technique that is illustrated below. There is more than one way to change a long whip, but the one shown here is probably the easiest.

1 Start by putting both the reins into the hand that is holding the stick, as you would if you were changing the short whip.

2 Turn the hand so the thumb goes down and the whip turns up. Turn the other hand, so that thumb is also turned down.

3 Take hold of the whip in the new hand and turn your hand back to the normal position.

4 Now put the reins back into both hands. You have smoothly changed the whip over.

Falling off

This is not something that any horse rider enjoys and, although the likelihood of it happening can be minimized, there is always a possibility that it can occur. However, if your riding school has good safety procedures in place and they work with you at a pace you feel comfortable with on horses who are suited to the tasks you are undertaking, there is less possibility of you hitting the ground.

Remember, however, that horses are living, thinking beings who are creatures of flight, so there is always the potential for something unexpected happening. Horses may trip over violently or shy suddenly at something that has caught their eye, and that might be all that is needed for you to lose your balance.

Get back on

A fall can easily shake your confidence, and it may make you question whether or not you wish to continue riding. If you have a fall and are definitely not injured, sometimes it helps to get right back on the horse, even if you just walk around afterward. If you feel that you do not want to get back on, that's fine – do not let anyone push you into it. Discuss with your instructor the reason for your fall and how, if possible, it could have been avoided. Talking it through with someone will help you to rationalize what happened, which, in turn, can help you to come to terms with it.

Try not to let a first fall put you off riding. Give it another go and take the pressure off yourself by doing some basic exercises in your next lesson. If you feel nervous and worried, you can take heart from the fact that most other people feel the same the first time they ride after a fall. In fact, it may take more than one lesson to start enjoying yourself again.

Lost your nerve?

Many people find that their desire to be with horses and their pleasure in riding them will eventually overcome their worry about falling off. If you really want to continue with your riding, but have "lost your nerve," either from falling off or for some other reason, try spending some time looking after horses, mucking out, grooming them and cleaning tack. Just being with them can help to build up your confidence again. Do not try to hide your worry – it will never get better like that.

Discuss it with your instructor and explain the way you feel. A good teacher will encourage you to continue and take you back as far as you need to go. Even if you have to go all the way back to having your teacher walk around with you, there is no need to feel that this is demeaning. As long as you continue to work at a level you are happy with, you will soon feel your confidence slowly returning. It will not be long before you get fed up with walking around and want to move on to something a little more exciting and challenging.

The most important thing is to keep it all within your stride. If the process is rushed, then you are unlikely to totally regain your confidence. The majority of riders have, at some time or another, lost all or part of their nerve, so do not imagine that you are any different and are expected to take it all in your stride.

Not for you?

If, after falling off, you feel riding is definitely not for you, then don't be afraid to admit it. Not everyone enjoys skiing or playing tennis, so it is not compulsory to enjoy horse riding. However, it is advisable to try again one more time after a fall before giving up completely.

Saddle comfort

Some people find it really difficult to be comfortable in the saddle. Saddles come in many shapes and designs, but you will probably learn to ride in a general purpose saddle, which is a compromise between a jumping and a dressage saddle.

Maintenance and safety

Saddles are extremely expensive items to purchase, and it is important that they are looked after carefully to keep them in good condition. Not only must they be cleaned regularly (see page 95) but they should also be put down correctly. They should never be left on a horse's back without the girth being done up, as the horse could shake himself and the tree could break if the saddle lands on the ground. So try to take good care of the school's investment.

The general purpose saddle is a compromise between the dressage and jumping saddles. It is a little more forward cut than a dressage saddle but not as much as the jumping saddle.

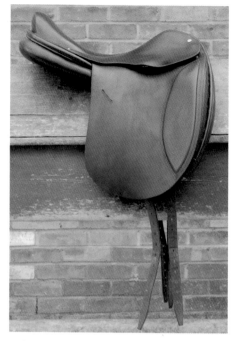

A dressage saddle has a fairly straight flap in front of your knee, often with long girth straps, so the buckles aren't under the knee.

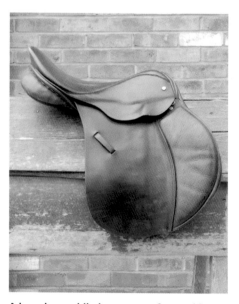

A jumping saddle has a more forward knee roll and a flatter cantle, so that your seat can move back in your jumping fold.

The right fit

The saddle you use must primarily fit the horse. If you are riding at a riding school, many different people will use the same saddle, but if you have your own horse, you can ensure that the saddle will fit both the horse and yourself. If you always feel uncomfortable in the saddle, talk it over with your instructor. It may be too small or too big for you. If the saddle is too big, you may well feel insecure; if it's too small you may feel very uncomfortable.

Of course, it may not be possible to find another saddle that fits both you and your horse, but if you change horses the new saddle could be just what is required.

The right saddle

Do not feel as though you are always asking your teacher questions or trying to monopolize her time. She should be prepared to talk things over with you and make adjustments wherever possible. A different saddle that fits you and the horse can make a huge difference to your security and position.

This saddle fits the horse and rider. The rider can sit comfortably in the middle with room to move if necessary.

This saddle is too small. The rider's bottom is almost off the back of the saddle.

This rider has very long legs and will encounter difficulties finding a saddle in which he can feel comfortable.

Checking your stirrup length

You may not always feel comfortable when you're learning to ride. You will be using muscles that you have forgotten you had, and there will be pressure on various parts of your anatomy. Your seat bones are a real pressure point, and you should always be able to feel them both equally when you are riding. If you cannot do so, check that your stirrups are level.

Level stirrups
This may seem obvious, but it's very easy to get in to the habit of having one stirrup longer than the other and eventually you will think they are level. Once you are a competent rider, your instructor may not check that your stirrups are level for you.

If the school has a mirror, take a look in that to see. Get into the habit of checking both stirrups against your out-straightened arm before you mount.

Checking the length
Another way to check your stirrup length once you are mounted is to check the position of your knees in relation to the knee roll of the saddle – are they both the same distance from the knee roll and

This rider (right) is not straight. Note how the left stirrup is longer than the right one. The rider (far right) is level, with her weight equally on her seat bones and the stirrups level.

do your knee joints feel bent the same amount? Counting the holes in the stirrup leathers is an unreliable way of telling whether they are level, as leather can stretch different amounts.

No excuses

As with jumping length stirrups, flatwork stirrups will alter for each individual rider, depending on their anatomy, the horse's size and the type of saddle they are using. People with very long thighs or lower legs may well have to compromise their riding position, but there is no excuse for not having their stirrups the same length. This must always be checked, whether you are just riding round in a school, out hacking or jumping.

This rider has a good stirrup length for performing any flatwork. Notice how the stirrup leather is hanging vertically. The rider appears to be comfortable.

This rider's stirrups are too long for the depth of seat, and she is reaching for them. Consequently, her foot is insecure in the stirrup.

A good position

Most rider problems stem from an insecure, poor position. Get your position checked every time you ride, even if you are only hacking out. Professional sports people have their own coaches to ensure that their bodies don't take the easy way out, and riding is no exception. We all need to be checked regularly.

Opposite: This horse and rider are enjoying themselves, working and practicing together in a ménage.

Are you one-sided?

When you are sitting in a chair or driving your car, see if you can feel both your seat bones equally. You may have a tendency to lean to one side without even knowing. If this is the case, think about the way you are sitting even when you are not on a horse. You may be surprised to learn how one-sided you are, and this will have an effect on the way your horse moves.

Mirror check

Another way to check that you are sitting level is to sit in front of a mirror and look at your shoulders. Are they level? Look at people on the television and around you – observe how many people do not sit with their weight equally distributed, so their shoulders are not the same height. It is not just a problem that you have. It is just that as a rider you need to work on improving your posture and weight distribution.

Practice makes perfect

Some people do not progress as quickly as they would wish, and this can be frustrating. Remember that riding is a sport and, while books can give you valuable guidance, there is nothing like practice to improve.

Make an effort

It is possible to "sit" on a horse and enjoy yourself, but you will never make genuine progress unless you put some effort in to what you are doing. This uses energy and takes mental concentration – just as in any new skill you choose to learn. Learning to ride is doubly difficult because there is another living being involved – the horse.

Be patient

Do not become frustrated if you do not feel that you are progressing as fast as you should. Riding well is an extremely difficult skill to master; in fact, many accomplished riders will tell you that they do not feel they are a "good rider" as there is always something new to learn. Nobody knows everything about riding and horses – this is one of the reasons why it is so fascinating. So keep an open mind and just go on practicing – you will get better and better.

You will improve

As you improve, your feel for what is going on underneath you will get better, and you will find you are starting to correct things your horse is thinking about doing before he actually does them. Although things will go wrong less and less frequently, there will always be the odd day when something does not work. Horses are not automatons and you must remember this. You will find that as you improve, you will gain more and more skills that will help you to build up a good relationship with any of the horses you ride. Then you will be well on the way to becoming an accomplished horse person.

Stay relaxed

Sometimes the more you try to analyze what you are doing, the worse it can get. This is because you will be trying so hard that you will lose your softness and will not be listening to what your horse is trying to tell you. If possible, try to stay relaxed and listen to your instructor. Different people have different learning styles, and some are more suited to riding than others.

Chapter 11

Looking after horses

Learning more about how to look after horses can be very satisfying as well as helping to improve your general fitness. There is not enough space here for an in-depth analysis of all aspects of stable management, so we will just look at the three most important ones: housing, grooming and feeding. By understanding more about a horse's needs, you will become more confident around them. This can aid your riding skills.

Living out at grass

A horse is naturally a herd animal that spends a great of deal of his time grazing and interacting with other horses. For these reasons, it is best for him to spend as much time as possible out in a field rather than being confined to a stall.

The generally accepted minimum acreage a horse can live on is one acre, although if he lives out all the year round, this may not be enough. If he spends part of his time in a stable and the remainder in a field, this will be easier for both of you.

Pasture management

Droppings in the field should always be picked up on a daily basis to prevent worm infestation and to encourage consistent grass growth. This is probably the most vital part of managing the field in which your horse lives, and although it is time consuming it will ensure that you have a well looked-after field, which will help to promote your horse's health.

Because horses poach the ground, weeds can take hold easily and will spread quickly if they are not controlled.

Checking the field

You should always check the field daily to make sure that all is well. If your horse lives out all year round, he should be checked at least twice a day. Keep an eye out, too, for any poisonous plants – ragwort can be a real problem in many areas. It is essential that you learn to recognize this and pull it up and burn it immediately. Remember that it is just as poisonous (and more palatable to horses) when it is dead. When you are pulling it out, make sure that you wear some protective gloves.

Know your poisons

Many plants are poisonous to horses. Learn to recognize them, using an illustrated plant guide, and check a new field before turning your horse out in it. If you find any poisonous plants, dig them up and burn them immediately. Trees and hedging material that are too big to be dug out must be cut back and securely fenced off.

Meadow plants

The most harmful meadow plants are ragwort, all the members of the nightshade family, meadow saffron, foxglove, hemlock, bracken, and monkshood. Aconite, bryony, flax, horseradish, hellebores, lupins, purple milk vetch, St. John's wort, water dropwort, and yellow star thistle are also dangerous.

Shrubs and trees

Poisonous shrubs include box, laurel, rhododendron, and privet. Among trees, even a small amount of yew usually proves fatal. Keep horses away from laburnum, and take care with oaks, whose leaves and acorns, if devoured in large quantities, are

Poached fields

Horses are notorious grazers. They can poach fields when they play with each other, and gate areas may become deep and boggy. If their droppings are left uncollected, then long, rank grass will grow that is unpalatable to them. To ensure their quality, fields must be maintained regularly.

These horses are grazing happily in a field surrounded by a thick hedge, which is protected by some wire fencing. Notice how the wire is tight and is well maintained.

Dead plants

Some poisonous plants, most notably ragwort and foxgloves, are more palatable to horses when they are dead, so never leave cuttings from any poisonous growth lying around. Do inspect your land regularly; it may start off being poison-free, but toxic plants can spread all too easily from adjacent fields.

harmful. If there is a good crop of acorns, rake them up and remove from the field; alternatively, completely fence off the tree to prevent horses accessing them.

Poisonous vegetation

Below are listed some of the plants that are harmful to horses. Look out for them. If horses do not have adequate grazing, they may well pick at them.

Acorns and crab apples Clear up and remove fallen crab apples from grazing pasture; they can cause severe colic. Acorns in large quantities are poisonous, but harmless in smaller amounts.

Bracken Horses eat this in late autumn or when other food is scarce. Bracken contains a chemical that destroys Vitamin

B1. It usually has to be consumed over several months before producing any recognizable symptoms.

Deadly nightshade The brown or purple berries are poisonous. It grows in hedges on the edges of fields and should be pulled out and burned.

Horsetail The effects of this plant, which is also sometimes known as "mare's tail," are similar to those of bracken. It is usually eaten in hay.

Milkweed, rhododendron, and foxglove These contain chemicals that affect the heart and can cause sudden death in a horse. Dig them up and dispose of them.

Water hemlock and hemlock The symptoms of nervous system poisoning appear within two hours of these plants being eaten by a horse.

Ragwort This will cause liver damage if it is consumed over weeks or months. It is usually found dried in hay, making it particularly dangerous. Its yellow flowers are in bloom between July and September, and mature plants can grow to a height of 4 feet (120 cm). You must pull up the plants and burn them.

Yew All parts of this tree are poisonous, even when it is dead. Just a handful of leaves, twigs, or berries can lead to fatal effects for a horse within a matter of minutes. Always make sure that there are no yew trees bordering the areas where you turn out your horse to graze.

Ragwort, with its very distinctive yellow flowers, is highly poisonous to horses. It attacks their liver.

Fencing

A field should always be securely fenced.
Post-and-rail fencing with a thick hedge
is the ideal, offering both security and
shelter for the horse. There are other forms
of acceptable boundaries, too, including
stud rails and stone walls. Electric tape
is excellent if it is used to split a field, but
it should not be used directly on to a road
side. Whatever type of fencing you use,
it must be checked regularly and properly
maintained. Never use wire mesh.

This post-and-rail fence
with a wooden gate is
practical, safe, and
looks very smart.

Some establishments
will run electric fence
along and post-and-rail
fence lines to stop
horses chewing the
wood, and discourage
play over the fence.

Thick hedges provide an
excellent natural barrier
and provide shelter.
They must be inspected
regularly for gaps and
poisonous plants.

Types of gate

It is vital that the gate is strong and has a secure catch. Gates can be made of wood or metal. Metal gates are cheaper but do not break if there is an accident of some sort. Keep gates well maintained, so they open and shut easily.

A metal sprung gate handle will require only one hand to open and close the gate.

Padlock a remote or isolated field to prevent people accidentally leaving the gate open.

Heavy-duty metal gates are suitable either with metal or with wooden posts. Treat them with a rust-resistant solution.

Water

The field should have a constant supply of water for the horse. An automatically-fed trough is ideal, but this can be expensive and is not always possible. A trough that is filled up regularly is fine, but it is hard work to keep it replenished – you will have to use a hose pipe or buckets. Buckets, by themselves as water containers, are not suitable, as horses will knock them over.

Siting containers

Any water container, whatever method you decide to use, should always be sited well away from any trees with falling leaves, and never in the corners of fields where horses can be trapped.

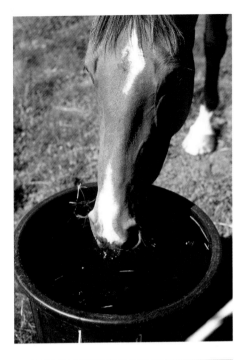

Buckets tend to be an unreliable way of providing continuous water as they can be knocked over easily, leaving horses without any water until you revisit them.

Keep any drinking troughs sited in your horse's field topped up regularly with plenty of clean, fresh water.

Skipping out

Try to get into a good habit of mucking out your horse's stall during the day, so he will not have to stand in his droppings and spread the manure around the stall. This will save you clean bedding and help ensure that he does not contract thrush (see page 189).

Mucking out

If your horse has his own stable and lives in part of the day, he will need mucking out daily. For this, you will need the following equipment: a wheelbarrow, a four-pronged fork, a shovel, a muck bucket, and a broom. Some people find that a two-pronged fork is easier for sorting and putting down the bed. Note that shavings and hemp beds will require specially designed forks.

Mucking out with the horse inside

It is always safer to muck out the stable when the horse is not inside the box. Not only is there less danger of him or you being injured, but also he will not be able to inhale any

of the dust that is disturbed while you are working and moving the bedding.

If you have to leave the horse inside the stall while you are mucking out, then tie him up securely and work around him. Safety is paramount, and you must not allow yourself on any account to become trapped in a corner of the stall. The horse must be prepared to move over for you when you put a hand on his quarters and say "over."

Fitness and safety

Mucking out is also a really good way of keeping yourself fit. Always try to work quickly and efficiently, ensuring that any tools that you are not using are leaned safely against the wall outside the stall.

1 Start off by removing all visible droppings. Put the muck bucket between your legs behind the droppings and flick them into the muck bucket.

2 With a fork, sort out the clean and dirty straw. Throw the clean straw against the wall, leaving the dirty straw in the middle of the box.

3 If you use a long-handled fork and keep one hand on the end, it will be easier for your back. If a horse is inside the stall while you are mucking out, it will prevent you prodding him.

4 Push all the bedding you wish to save to one side of the stall. Pile up the wet bedding in a wheelbarrow. Sweep the floor, shoveling the sweepings into the wheelbarrow.

Making banks

If you need some more bedding for the center of the bed, it is best to use the bank from the side and then make new banks with clean straw. These will keep your horse warm and help prevent him from getting cast – when he tries to roll and gets stuck on his back.

5 If you stack the wheelbarrow by filling the corners first and then the middle, you will get more sweepings in than if you just pile them up in the center like this one.

6 If you can leave the bedding up for a while, the floor can dry out. If not, put it down with either the two-prong or four-prong fork, lifting, not dragging, the straw.

Looking after equipment

No matter whether you are just brushing off or bathing a horse, always keep your equipment together and tidy, so you don't lose any items. If your horse stepped on the equipment he could lame himself. Wash your grooming kit regularly with soapy water and make sure you turn the brushes bristles down so they can dry and will not rot.

Grooming

This vital procedure has many important functions. It helps to keep your horse's skin healthy, improves his muscle tone, aids in building a bond between the two of you, and it also makes the horse look nice and feel more comfortable.

Dandy brush
The long, stiff bristles will remove dried mud and sweat. The dandy brush may be used on the horse's body if he has not been clipped, but it is too harsh for a thin-coated horse, one who has sensitive skin, or for use on the horse's head. It is not suitable for the mane and tail as it will break the hairs.

Water brush
The bristles of the water brush, which are shorter and softer than those of a dandy brush, are used for dampening the mane and tail. It can also be used to remove stable stains (where a horse has lain in his droppings). You can use a dry water brush to remove any mud and sweat from a sensitive-skinned horse.

Metal curry comb
The teeth of the metal curry comb are used for cleaning the body brush. You simply draw the brush over the teeth after every few strokes and tap the dirt out of the curry comb at regular intervals well away from the horse. The metal curry comb should never be used on the horse.

Mane and tail combs
These metal or plastic combs are not required for grooming, although they are essential items when you want to pull (thin and trim) or plait a horse's mane or tail.

Body brush
The short, fine bristles of the body brush can be used all over the horse, including his legs, head, mane, and tail. This brush is fitted with a loop through which you can slip your hand.

Sweat scraper
The scraper's rubber blade, attached to a metal frame, is used to remove excess water from the horse's coat after he has been washed down. Be careful when working on bony areas.

Plastic curry comb
The teeth of this comb are suitable for removing dried mud from the coat of an unclipped horse.

Rubber curry comb
This is used for removing mud, sweat, and any loose hairs from the coat as well as for massaging the horse.

Cactus cloth
This coarse-weave cloth can be used instead of a plastic curry comb for removing mud and sweat.

Grooming tools

A wide variety of equine grooming tools can now be purchased at most saddlers. Here you can see some of the most common ones and their uses. Each tool has its own special function.

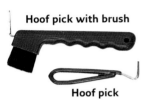

Hoof pick with brush

Hoof pick

Hoof pick
The hoof pick, which must have a blunt end to avoid causing injury, is used to clean soil, droppings, stones, etc., from the horse's feet.

Sponges
Sponges are used for cleaning the horse's eyes, nostrils, and dock (area under his tail). Always keep separate sponges for the head and dock.

Bucket
This is useful for washing a horse's feet, and also for wetting sponges and water brushes. Never use this for his drinking water.

Stable rubber
Use a cloth stable rubber slightly damp to remove the last vestiges of dust from the coat and give it a gloss at the end of grooming.

Other equipment
There are some other items of equipment that might prove extremely useful when you are grooming a horse, and these include the grooming tools shown below.

Pulling comb
This is used both to tidy and shorten manes and strip out long hairs.

Hoof brush
This small brush is good to use when washing the horse's hooves.

Hoof oil brush
This is used for oiling horses' hooves. It is only done on special occasions.

Brushing off a grass-kept horse

The majority of people tend to groom their horses just to make them look neat and tidy and this is called brushing off or, for a stabled horse, quartering (see page 171).

Picking out the feet

Always start grooming a horse by picking out his feet. Pick them out into a bucket to help keep the yard or stable tidy.

Brushing

For a horse who lives out, it is important not to take too many of the essential oils from his skin as these are needed to help protect him from the elements. If he is very muddy, a plastic curry comb followed by the dandy brush will remove the worst of the mud and make him look respectable. Always use a body brush or your fingers to go through the mane and tail – other brushes will take out too much hair.

When picking out a horse's feet, always work from the heel towards the toe of the foot. Do take special care not to damage the frog (the triangle-shaped part of the foot). Stand close to the horse and face backward.

When picking out a hind foot, make sure you hold underneath the horse's leg. If your arm is over his leg and he kicks out, he could damage your arm. Place the bucket under his foot to collect the debris.

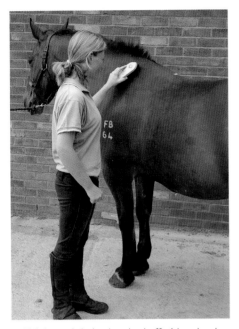

1 This horse is being brushed off with a dandy brush. Always stand facing the hindquarters, so you will be aware if he is going to kick.

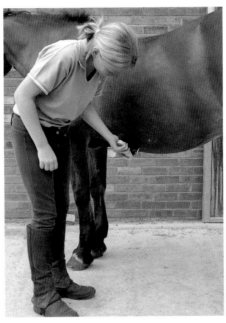

2 Brush firmly or you may tickle the horse and annoy him. Ensure the girth area underneath is free from mud, or he could get a girth gall.

Brushing the tail

When brushing a tail with a body brush or your fingers, stand to the side of the horse and hold the whole tail, letting out just a few hairs at a time and untangling them.

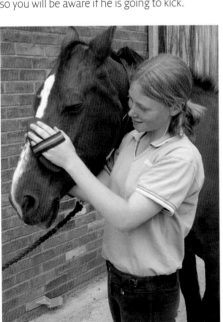

3 Use a soft body brush for the head. Undo the quick-release knot, leaving the rope through the tie ring. Fasten the halter around his neck.

4 Put the mane to the other side of the neck, brush under it with a body brush, then bring it back over and brush the top. Dampen if needed.

Brushing the head

When you brush your horse's head you must be very careful. It is advisable to use a body brush for this. Be gentle, as it is easy to make your horse "head shy" if you are too rough. Undo the lead rope and just put the rope through the string – then if he pulls back he will not injure himself. Put the halter around his neck, so you still have control but his head is easy to brush. As with all grooming, follow the lie of the coat and brush firmly, but carefully. You can sponge his eyes, nose, and dock to refresh him and to help keep infection at bay.

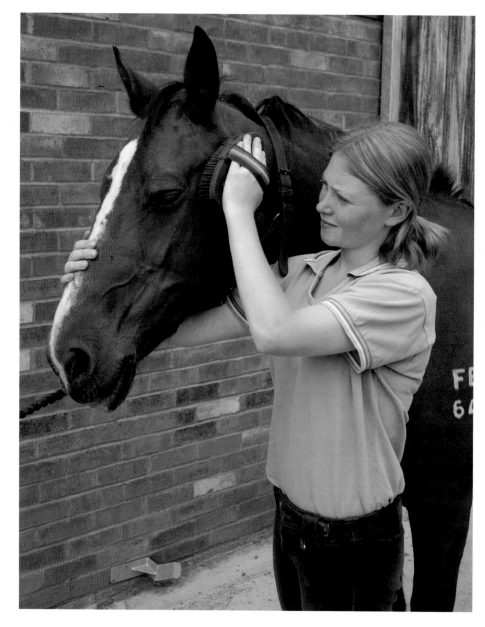

This horse is looking relaxed about having his head groomed. Control is maintained throughout by keeping the halter around his neck and a hand over his nose. The body brush is used firmly but sympathetically.

Quartering a stabled horse

The only difference between quartering a stabled horse and brushing off a grass-kept one (see page 168) is that you will use the body brush in conjunction with the curry comb instead of the dandy brush. If your horse has any stable stains (where he has been lying in his droppings), these can be washed off easily with a bucket of water and a water brush. Try not to get the horse too wet. However, if this does happen, it is advisable to towel the area dry, so he is less likely to catch a chill or get stiff.

Cleaning the dock

It is always best to use a different sponge for cleaning the dock. Stand to one side of the horse's rear, lift the tail out of the way, and work quickly and efficiently.

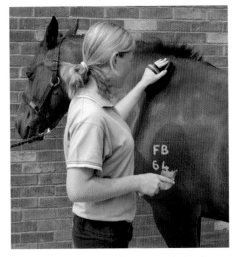

1 With a body brush and curry comb, brush two or three long strokes with the lie of the coat.

2 Run the curry comb through the brush to take out the loose hair and scurf.

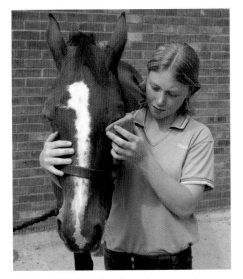

3 Control the head and gently sponge the eyes. Wash out the sponge after each eye.

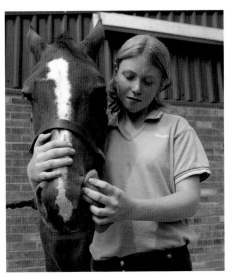

4 Sponge the nostrils to remove dust and dirt and minimize the risk of respiratory problems.

Strapping

A thorough groom is called strapping, and
this process can take up to 45 minutes to
complete. You typically strap a show horse
who lives in a stable most of the time.

1 You start strapping with the rubber curry
comb in a circular motion all over his body
to loosen the hair and dead skin.

2 Next, use the body brush in conjunction
with the metal curry comb. Try to get in a
good rhythm and use the brush once or
twice before cleaning it with the curry comb.

3 When you have done this all over the
horse, you can gently bang him. While not
a routine part of grooming, this builds up
muscle and must not be done on the bony
parts of his body. Do it on his neck muscles
and the muscles of his quarters. Again,
you need to build up a rhythm. Bang the
massage pad onto the muscle, slide it along
his skin a little, and then wipe with the stable

rubber. If you do this rhythmically a few
times on the same muscle, you will see the
muscle contract ready for the bang and this
is what helps to build up the muscle mass.

Feeding and diet

Feeding your horse properly is a real art. In
the last few years, a great deal of research
has been undertaken, and the science
behind feeding is now better understood.
Some feeding rules provide sound
guidance, and if you follow the ones
outlined below they will help you to
maintain your horse's fitness and health.

Feed according to the individual
The most important rule of all is to feed
according to your horse's size, the work
being done, his temperament and age, and
the time of year. If you feed your horse too
much, you will change his behavior and

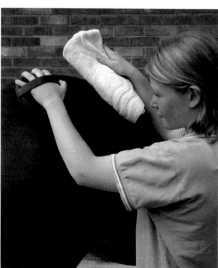

1 Banging with a massage pad and stable
rubber helps to build up muscle. The horse
must be introduced to this process carefully.

2 After banging the pad or wisp, wipe the area
with a stable rubber to help boost circulation
and obtain a consistent rhythm.

possibly make him more difficult to ride and control. You can also induce health problems, such as filled legs. Alternatively, if you do not feed him enough, he will lose weight and will not be able to undertake the work you want him to do.

You must decide how much feed your horse needs every day. He needs two-and-a-half percent of his body weight daily to maintain his health and condition. This may come as 100 percent bulk food, such as grass or hay, if he is doing little or no work. The amount of hard/concentrate food, such as grain or oats, that you feed him per day will depend on how much work he is doing. As a rough guide, a horse doing approximately

one hour's light work of hacking and/or simple schooling a day will require between 10 and 20 percent of his feed a day to be provided in the form of concentrates.

You may need to feed a little more grain during the winter months, but if your horse is doing less work than in the summer this may not be the case. Look carefully at your horse and always note his behavior and body condition.

Feed small amounts often

In the wild, your horse is a "trickle feeder." His stomach is very small for his body size and he is unable to cope with large amounts of feed at a time. If he has free access to

Feeding regimes

There is a huge array of concentrate feed on the market for horses. This can be very confusing. Most feed companies will offer advice on their products and how to feed them. The acid test is your horse's condition and behavior. Every horse is an individual, and what one horse needs to maintain his work level may be different to another one living in the same field. Consequently, it is not a good idea to compare horses' feed regimes.

This horse has access to ad lib hay. He is in good condition and is content to be in his stable.

Want to know more?

This section has only touched on the basic rules of feeding. There are many books on this subject that go into more detail should you wish to know more.

grass or, in his stable, hay or haylage, he will learn not to gorge his food. Ad lib bulk food prevents him becoming bored if he is stabled for several hours a day. If he is greedy, access to grass or hay may need to be restricted. If he is fed little and often with regard to his hard feed, this is closer to the way in which he feeds in the wild.

Feed plenty of bulk

Your horse's digestive system needs bulk to keep it working. If you cut his bulk down too much, there is a possibility of digestive and psychological problems. By giving your horse plenty of bulk in his diet, you are mimicking his natural life style.

Feed good-quality food

If you feed poor-quality food, it can be cheaper, but it will be a false economy. He may well not eat it (some horses are very fussy feeders), or if he does he may have

This horse has a manger for his concentrate food. Some people believe that it is better to feed all food on the floor as this is the natural position for a horse to eat.

digestive problems, such as colic. Feeding dusty hay can lead to respiratory problems, so make sure you feed the best-quality food that you can afford to buy.

Horses are very fond of their grain, and it should be fed to them at regular times and as quickly as possible to avoid bad habits.

Feed at regular times

A horse is a creature of habit and lives and works best when he has a regular routine. He may become unsettled if he does not have one. Work out a system for feeding hard food at regular times.

Clean feeding utensils

You would not like to eat your food from a dirty plate, and a dirty feed bowl can put your horse off eating. Mixing his food with a dirty spoon can also spread disease or cause food contamination, so always ensure that any feeding utensils are clean.

Constant access to water

A horse should have constant access to clean, fresh water, so he does not need to drink a lot of water after a hard feed. If he is kept in a field, an automatically filled trough is the best way to ensure this. Some stalls have automatic waterers in a corner and, if correctly maintained, they are an excellent way of ensuring your horse has free access to water. If these are not available, then buckets are fine, although some horses are prone to knocking them over. Buckets will need to be secured either by putting them in a tire (which can take up a lot of space in the stall) or by attaching them to the wall by a clip.

Feed succulents every day

A horse who lives in a field with good-quality grazing will get succulents daily. A stabled horse will enjoy spending some time in a field and perhaps some apples and/or carrots to supplement the grazing. This helps ensure he gets the vitamins and minerals he needs and also provides a treat.

Do not feed just before exercise

Do not give a horse a hard feed for at least an hour before riding him. His stomach will be full and this will press on his lungs and diaphragm and make it difficult for him to perform. If he lives in a field it is useful if you can bring him in to his stable for at least half an hour before you ride him. If this is not possible, make sure that you do not undertake any strenuous work at the beginning of your ride.

These horses and ponies have access to adequate grazing. They are all in good condition physically and mentally.

Chapter 12

What next?

Now that you are a reasonably competent rider, you may feel ready to move on to new equestrian challenges. There are so many options from which to choose, some of which are outlined in this chapter. Many people feel that they need their own horse if they are to progress. Discuss this with your riding school and get professional advice. Confident riders may want to try competing in a major equine discipline, such as dressage, show jumping, or cross-country. You could also try endurance riding or eventing; there is so much to choose from.

Buying a horse

You may decide that, now you are making progress and improving as a rider, you want to own your own horse. This is many people's dream, but it is not a decision to be taken lightly, and you should never rush into buying a horse. Consider all the implications and expense carefully.

Responsibility and expense

Owning a horse is a huge responsibility, and sometimes it can feel as if you are throwing money around as if there is no tomorrow. Not only will you have to feed and house your horse, but there will be regular farrier's fees and vet's bills, too, although, hopefully, not too often.

Buying a horse can be a very trying experience. You need to decide on what you want to do with him, e.g. hacking out or competing in one of the many available equestrian disciplines, and also how much money you have to spend. Remember that in addition to the actual purchase price of the horse, you may also have to buy tack (saddle, bridle, etc.), rugs, grooming tools and many other items of equipment to go with him, and these can be expensive. If you're thinking of competing, you may even have to invest in a horse trailer.

Finding a horse

You can spend a long time looking for the right horse for you, but the important thing to remember is that the perfect horse rarely exists and what you will end up purchasing will usually be a compromise. Try not to buy the first horse you see –

there are many horses for sale out there. Equine magazines, the Internet, and the local press all have horses for sale, but the best way of all to find a horse is by word of mouth. Ask your horsey friends, your riding instructor, and the staff at the riding school if they know of any suitable horses for sale.

What to ask

When you phone up about a horse for sale, have a list of questions ready to ask. Don't be afraid to ask them – the more you know about the horse, the better prepared you are, and this is a good way of finding out whether it is worth your while going to see him. You want to confirm the following:
- The horse's age.
- His height, color, and sex.
- His breed.
- His temperament.
- That he really can do everything the advertisement says he can, e.g. what types of work can he do?
- Has he been successful in competition if you are planning to compete with him?
- Is he good in traffic if you are planning to ride on the road?
- Check whether he has any vices, such as weaving, crib-biting, wind-sucking.
- How long he has been owned by the current owner and who were the previous owners, if any.
- Is the horse currently turned out or stabled?
- What sort of feed does he have?
- Find out if the horse has been lame in the past, and what the condition and treatment were.
- Has the current owner ever made a claim on the horse's insurance?
- Would he pass a vet's inspection?

Viewing a horse

If you decide to go and see a horse, then do make sure that you arrive on time. If somebody is trying to sell a horse, it can be frustrating waiting around for hours for a prospective purchaser to arrive. Do not go to view the horse if you think he will not be suitable for you. You can avoid wasted visits by asking the current owner the questions listed on page 178. If possible, always take an experienced horse person with you to offer advice and expertise.

Observing the horse

Look at the horse in his stall first. Does he appear quiet and friendly? Ask the owner to pick up a front and a back foot and watch the horse's reaction. Observe him being tacked up – does he accept being tacked up as normal? Ask the owner to lead the horse out and trot him up for you on a hard surface – look for any signs of lameness. Watch him being ridden by the owner before you try him yourself. Ride the horse and, if you feel it is safe to do so, try him out on the road as well.

Take your time

If, at any time, you do not feel he is the right horse for you, then say so. The owner would rather know than you waste their time. You do not have to make a decision there and then, even if the seller tells you they have two other people coming later in the day – go away and think about it.

Take a knowledgeable person with you when viewing a horse. Get somebody to walk and trot him up.

Vetting the horse

If you decide to go ahead and buy the horse, it is always advisable to have him checked over by the vet. A five-stage vetting is the most thorough inspection that a vet will undertake. This will ensure that the horse is capable of doing the job you want him to do. If you buy a horse as a safe hack, it is not reasonable to expect him to turn in to a successful eventer two years later when you feel more confident as a rider and want to branch out into other equestrian disciplines.

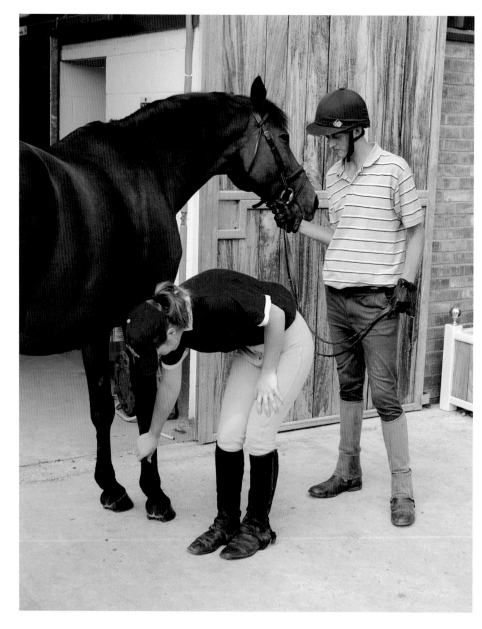

Ask an experienced person to check the horse's legs to ensure there are no major lumps or bumps and he is happy being handled.

Housing your horse

If you do decide to buy your own horse, you need to consider where you will keep him. This decision should be made before you actually purchase a horse. You may be lucky enough to have your own facilities with a paddock and a stable, or be able to rent one nearby. This will mean you need to find the time to attend to your horse at least twice a day – in the morning and the evening – and also have time to ride him. Some people find they spend all their time attending to their horse and only get to ride him at weekends.

Boarding

You may decide that the best solution for your situation is to keep your horse at a boarding stable. Ideally, this could be the same place as your riding school.

Pasture boarding

Pasture boarding is the cheapest option, but, again, you will need the time to look after your horse yourself. If you can build up good relationships with other people at the barn, then you may be able to share the stable management tasks. In a pasture boarding situation you usually pay for the

If you keep your horse at a riding school or other boarding facility, there will usually be members of the staff to lend a hand if help is required.

181

use of a field and possibly a small lock-up area, too – you will have to provide everything else.

Some facilities are adamant that you must buy all your feedstuffs from them and will insist upon you maintaining your horse on their worming program. Read the small print of the contract very carefully and be sure that you are willing to abide by all the rules and regulations. A barn that has no rules may seem a more acceptable alternative but, if a barn is to run smoothly with the horses' best interests at heart, some regulation will be necessary. It is just a matter of finding a happy medium that you can live with.

You need to ensure that you have the time to look after your horse, regardless of where you board.

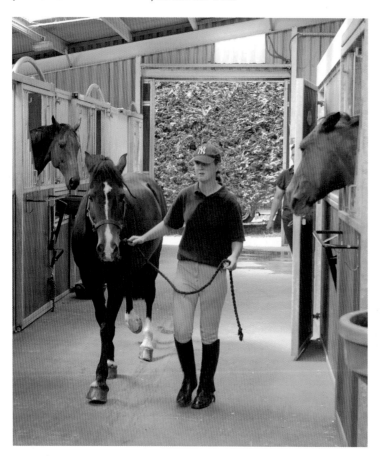

Full board

You may decide that you do not have the time to take care of your horse yourself. If so, you should consider full board, where all the stable management your horse requires is undertaken for you. Exercise and/or schooling may also be provided when you are unable to ride, but this may add to the cost. Full board is not a cheap option, and some people find they do not develop a really satisfying relationship with their horse because they are not spending much time with him. It all depends on what suits you.

Working board

A middle-of-the-road option is what is called working board. This is where you keep your horse at a riding school, which will be able to use your horse for an agreed number of hours a week. In return for this, you get all your horse's stable management requirements at a reduced rate. This has the advantage of keeping your horse schooled and exercised as well for a reasonable sum.

Before deciding on this option, however, you should read the small print of the contract very carefully. Some matters, such as who pays vets' fees (especially if the horse is injured when he is being ridden by a riding school client) and who replaces lost or broken tack, need to be taken into consideration. If you have a really good relationship with your riding school, then this can be a useful type of agreement. However, as with all types of boarding, you must have a contract, so that both sides know exactly what their rights and responsibilities are.

Leasing horses

Some riding schools run schemes whereby riders can lease horses from them. This can be a useful scheme, and it will enable you to get a feel of what is required if you own a horse without you having to go through the heartache of having to sell your horse should it not work out.

Other riding schools may let you hire horses by the day to attend pleasure rides or go to competitions. A pleasure ride is a marked ride over a rural area which will usually take about two hours to complete. You can go by yourself, but it is more enjoyable to ride with others. There is usually a small charge to go on the ride, and you will be counted out and back in to make sure you complete it safely.

This can be a really enjoyable experience, although you need to watch out for people who do not have good equine manners and can come galloping past you, upsetting your horse.

Riding clubs

Why not consider joining a local riding club? They typically run training, social events and competitions from local to national level. This is a great way to make like-minded friends and to share equine experiences.

Riding in open country, whether by yourself or with a group of friends, is not only an excellent way to relieve stress but also to exercise you and your horse.

Have a go!

Why not have a go at one of the following disciplines? You can try dressage, show jumping, eventing, Western riding, driving, vaulting, mounted games, polo, and endurance riding. All require different aspects of equine skill. However, if you are not competitive, just enjoy your horse.

Competitions

As your expertise and confidence grow, you may start thinking about competition – a local show can give you your first taste. It is a good idea to go to a show without your horse in the first instance as you can then see what happens without worrying about looking after him. There will be showing classes, both in hand and ridden, as well as jumping and, perhaps, dressage classes.

Which classes?

The first time you take your horse to a show, you need not necessarily enter any classes. Just ride him around so he gets used to seeing the sights and everything that is going on around you both. When you do enter some classes, do not put your name down for too many, otherwise you will spend your whole time dashing from one ring to another. Remember that we do all this for enjoyment, not to hasten our demise! You can always increase the number of classes you enter as you and your horse become more proficient.

Competitions are not for everybody. Some people see them as an essential part of their riding, but if you are not happy about them, then do not be pressurized by others. There is nothing wrong with just enjoying your horse at home.

Dressage competitions provide the opportunity to have your horse's level of schooling judged and assessed by a knowledgeable person.

There are many different obstacles you may encounter during the third phase of a TREC competition.

TREC

This is a rapidly growing discipline and is very popular with those riders who do not wish to specialize in one of the three major disciplines of show jumping, dressage or eventing. There are four levels of TREC, each of which has three sections, and points are awarded for each task.
• The first section is orienteering on horseback.
• The second section is where you have to ride a slow canter and then a fast walk over a certain distance.

• The third section is similar to an obstacle course on horseback. You may have to jump cross-country fences, go over a bridge, up a staircase, under low branches, or make your horse stand without you in a marked circle – the possibilities are numerous. If there are some tasks you do not want to do, you are not eliminated but you just do not receive the points.

Many people find that at the lower levels of TREC they are competing more against themselves than against other riders, and, consequently, they enjoy the whole experience hugely.

Opposite: What could be more enjoyable than cantering safely across open countryside on a well-schooled horse?

Showing your horse

Not everyone who rides is interested in showing their horse. Competition can be stressful and expensive. However, competing in horse shows, and dressage shows in particular, are a good way to gauge your progress and success as a rider. Besides being a lot of fun, riding in a show can help you gain valuable confidence. Attending shows also offers you an opportunity to watch and learn from other riders. Everyone who rides should try out at least one or two shows, just to see if they like it.

Many riding schools and clubs organize and sponsor local shows, so chances are you'll have no trouble finding one in your area. Usually, riding schools permit their students to show on school horses. In addition, most riding instructors encourage their students to start out at local schooling shows. They will help you select the appropriate classes, complete the

necessary entry forms, and prepare for your first exciting show day. So give it a go! Who knows, you may catch horse show fever and end up getting hooked.

Dressage shows

At most horse shows, a number of horses and riders enter the ring at the same time to trot their stuff. But dressage shows differ in that only you and your horse enter the ring to perform a prescribed test in front of the judge. Proficiency in dressage is divided into and scored at various levels, ranging from the introductory level through Grand Prix. Each level is comprised of a series of increasingly difficult dressage tests, which determine whether horse and rider are ready to move up to the next higher level. Most local shows test only at the lower levels, which go through fourth level. Because training progresses up each level, and each level builds on the other, your ability to execute each test and your scores are a relatively reliable measure of your progress. Often, the judge's comments on your tests provide good information on areas where you need to improve. To learn more about how horse shows in America are organized and governed, read the *Rule Book* published and updated annually by USEF, the United States Equestrian Federation.

Equestrian vacations

Many people enjoy going on an equestrian vacation, and there is now a wide range of places within the U.S. and overseas that specialize in riding vacations and can offer you instruction and/or hacking in beautiful

surroundings on quality horses. If your dream has always been to ride a horse along a beach and into the water, you now have the skills, so why not try it?

The best way to find the center you require is by word of mouth, or through a specialist company.

Finally...
This book has been designed to assist you in learning to ride safely and successfully.

The whole route is very much a three-way process – you, your horse, and your coach. Confidence between the three of you is vital for progression. Finding a riding school to suit you is also crucial. Remember that we never stop learning to ride, and even when you are proficient and confident an occasional lesson will ensure that you are not slipping into bad habits. Finally, always bear in mind that we ride horses to enjoy ourselves, so go out and have fun.

Useful addresses

American Riding Instructors Association (ARIA)
28801 Trenton Court
Bonita Springs, FL 34124-3337
(239) 948-3232
Web site: *www.riding-instructor.com*

U.S. Pony Clubs, Inc.
4041 Iron Works Parkway
Lexington, KY 40511
(859) 254-7669
Web site: *www.ponyclub.org*

United States Dressage Federation (USDF)
4051 Iron Works Parkway
Lexington, KY 40511
(859) 971-2277
Web site: *www.usdf.org*

United States Equestrian Federation (USEF)
4047 Iron Works Parkway
Lexington, KY 40511
(859) 258-2472
Web site: *www.usef.org*

Glossary

Action The way in which a horse moves.

Bay Brown color body with black mane, tail, and lower legs.

Blaze A broad white stripe running down the face.

Boarding facility An establishment providing paying accommodation for horses.

Cantle The back of the saddle.

Cavesson A piece of equipment made of leather or nylon worn by the horse when he is being lunged. The lunge line attaches to the metal ring on the nose piece.

Chestnut Ginger – red color of the body and mane and tail.

Cob A weight carrying type of small horse, usually with a good temperament.

Concentrates Food for horses other than grass, hay, or haylage. Often pre-prepared, ensuring a complete balanced feed.

Core stability The strength of the trunk area of your body.

Cribbing or crib-biting A "stable vice" whereby a bored horse grabs something with his teeth and takes in air.

Diagonal The way in which a horse moves in trot with opposite pairs of legs moving one after the other.

Diagonals In rising trot, the rider sits as the outside front leg and inside hind leg are on the ground.

Dressage The art of training a horse, so that he becomes obedient and responsive to the rider.

Drop and cross your stirrups Take your feet out of the stirrups and cross them over onto the horse's shoulders, so you can ride without stirrups.

Dun Yellowish or cream body color with black mane, tail, and lower legs.

Equitation The art of horse riding and horsemanship.

Flatwork Working and schooling a horse where no jumping is involved.

Fold The position taken by the rider as the horse jumps over a fence.

Forehand Front part of the horse, including the head, neck, shoulders, and forelegs.

Frog The "V" shaped part of the sole of the horse's foot that acts as a shock absorber and helps blood circulation.

Gelding A castrated male horse.

Girth gall A sore area in the girth region, caused by friction or a dirty girth.

Gray Any color horse from pure white to dark gray.

Grazing Grass fields for horses to live on and eat the grass down.

Grooming kit The various brushes and tools that are used to clean a horse.

Hack Going out for a ride, trail riding.

Hand The traditional unit of measurement for horses and ponies which is equivalent to 4 inches (10 cm).

Hock Joint in the center of the hind leg.

Impulsion Powerful, controlled forward movement.

Irons Stirrup irons attached to the saddle by stirrup leathers in which the rider's feet are placed.

Kind eye The horse's eye looks gentle, friendly, and interested in what is going on.

Knee rolls The front padded part of the saddle flaps. The knee lies behind them.

Lunge The horse works on a circle with the teacher holding a long lunge line attached to a lunge cavesson on the horse's head. A long lunge whip is held to encourage the horse forward.

Mare A female horse.

Martingale An attachment that goes through the girth and attaches to a part of the bridle to prevent the horse putting his head above the point of control.

Mucking out The daily task of cleaning out the stable, taking out the dirty bedding, and making the bed tidy and comfortable.

Near side The horse's left side.

Neckstrap A strap, usually made out of leather, that is attached round a horse's neck for a rider to hold should they need help with their balance.

Off side The horse's right side.

Palomino A gold or cream colored horse with a white mane or tail.

Piebald: A black and white paint horse.

Poached When fields are very wet, the area around the gateway and water trough becomes very muddy and churned up.

Points of the horse The names of each part of the horse.

Poll The point at the top of the horse's head immediately behind the ears.

Pommel Raised front part of the saddle.

Post Rising up and down in the saddle. This is usually in rising trot, sometimes done in the canter.

Rising trot Action of the rider rising from the saddle in rhythm with the horse's trot.

Roan A color produced from a mixture of white and any other colored hair distributed over the horse's body.

Saddle pad A pad used under the saddle to help keep the saddle clean and absorb sweat, shaped to fit the saddle.

Saddle soap Specially prepared soap to keep leather saddlery clean and supple.

Shy When a horse is "spooked" by something and moves quickly to one side.

Side reins Two pieces of leather attached from the girth to the bit rings used when lunging to help control the horse.

Skewbald Any other two-color paint other than black and white.

Skull cap A form of riding helmet that usually has a colored silk over it. Often worn for cross-country jumping.

Snaffle The commonest type of bit that usually has a ring at each side. A mild bit.

Sock White pastern and fetlock.

Star A white patch on the forehead.

Strapping A complete, thorough grooming of the horse.

Thrush A disease of the frog that is often associated with poor foot hygiene.

Transition The act of changing pace. From a slower pace to a faster pace is an upward transition. From a faster pace to a slower pace is a downward transition.

Turn out To put a horse out in a field.

Weaving A "stable vice" whereby a bored, stabled horse rocks his head and neck from side to side stereotypically.

Wind-sucking A "stable vice" whereby a horse will gulp in air without grasping something with his teeth (see cribbing).

Withers The highest point on the horse's back at the base of the neck. The pommel of the saddle fits over them.

Index

Acorns 160
Aids 37, 51, 52, 56, 102, 108, 144
Alexander Technique 144
Approaching horses 30
Arena diagram 72
Armchair position 64
Artificial aids 52
Balance 29, 30, 48, 52, 66, 71, 74, 76, 79, 104, 106, 108, 136, 144
  improving 117
Bay horses 38
Bedding 164
Bit 86, 87, 93, 94, 95, 96
Body protectors 8
Boots 24
Bounce 136
Bracken 160
Bridle 45, 82, 85
  cleaning 94
  putting on 86–89
  putting together 96–97
  taking off 93
Buckets 163, 175
Buckle guard 43, 48
Buying a horse 178–180
Calf muscles 58
Cantering 100–107, 108, 116, 124, 132
Classical position 30
Clothing 8, 22–25
  high-visibility 112
Competitions 184
Concentrates 173
Core stability 29, 144
Crab apples 160
Cross pole jumps 126
Deadly nightshade 160

Depth of seat 144
Diagonals 70–72, 100
Diet 172–175
Direct transition 108
Dismounting 52
Downwards transition 108
Dressage 184
  saddle 150
Drinking troughs 163
Electric fencing 161
Exercises, fitness 26–29, 52, 77, 124
Falling off 149
Feeding a horse 172–175
Feel, improving 108
Feet, picking out 40, 168
Fences 132, 136
Fencing 17, 161
Fetlock bands 112
Fields 17, 158–161, 175
  poached 159
Fitness 26–29, 52, 77, 124
Flexibility 26–29
Footwear 24
Forward seat 121
Foxglove 160
Gates 162
General-purpose saddle 150
Girth 43, 58, 60, 85, 90, 91, 92, 102, 114, 150
  checking 43, 47, 48
Gloves 25, 41, 112, 113, 158
Grazing 17, 35, 158–161, 175
Gridwork 132, 136–139
Grooming 149, 166–172
  tools 166–167
Group lessons 19, 72

Hacking out 30, 70, 111–117
Half-halt 108
Halt 59, 124
Halter 41, 83, 86, 170
Hedges 161
Helmets 8, 22–23, 41
Hemlock 160
High-visibility clothing 112
Holidays 186
Horsetail 160
Indoor schools 12
Instructors 14–15, 52, 100, 149
Jodhpurs 24, 95
Jumping 119–139, 184
  positions 121, 136
  saddle 150
Kicking 16, 115
Lead rein 18, 52
Leading a horse 34, 40–42, 52
Leasing horses 183
Lessons 18–19, 72
  first 33–53
  lunge 18, 19, 106, 144
Light hands 57, 59
Light seat 121, 122–124, 126
Livery 9, 181–182
Long whips 146
  changing 148
  using 148
Lunge lessons 18, 19, 144
  for canter 106
Martingale 41, 85, 189
Milkweed 160
Mounting 41, 44, 45–47, 114
  blocks 45, 47
Mouth 86, 94, 123

Moving forward 58

Mucking out 149, 164–165

Muscles 26, 58, 77, 102

Neckstrap 50, 59, 63, 64, 78, 102, 124

One stride double 132

Passing the rear of the ride 142, 143, 144

Pasture management 158

Pleasure rides 183

Poached fields 159

Points of the horse 38–39

Poisonous plants 158–160

Pole work 123, 124–125

Post-and-rail fencing 161

Posture 51, 65, 78, 154

Pressure points 90, 91, 152

Progressive transition 108

Qualifications 186

Quartering 171

Quick-release knots 84–85, 86

Ragwort 158, 160

Reflective bands 112

Reins 41, 45, 50, 52, 56–57, 59, 63, 78, 106, 122–123
  changing 62, 72, 106, 147

Relaxing exercises 77

Rhododendron 160

Riding clubs 183

Riding position 51–52, 58, 65, 74, 78, 144, 154
  classical 30, 51

Riding schools 8, 11–19

Rising trot 63, 65, 66–67, 79, 104, 124
  diagonals in 72

Road work 112

Saddle 39, 43, 45, 46, 49, 63, 65, 82, 85, 102
  cleaning 95
  comfort 150–151
  puttting on 90–91
  soap 94–95
  taking off 92

Saddle pads 90, 91

Safety 8, 40, 41, 43, 150, 164
  quick-release knots 84–85
  on roads 8, 112, 114

Short whips 146
  changing 147
  using 146–147

Sitting trot 52, 63, 64–65, 102
  diagonals in 71

Snaffle bridle, putting together 96–97

Stable door, securing 42

Stable management 34, 82, 164–175, 186

Stiffness 144

Stirrup(s) 41, 43, 46, 51, 52, 64, 114, 120
  altering 49
  checking 44, 47
  cleaning 95
  leathers 96, 153
  length 152–154
  loops 49
  riding without 74–79

Stopping 59

Strapping 172

Stretching 26–29, 77, 124

Stud rails 161

Succulents 175

Suppleness 52, 78

Suspension 63, 100

Tack, cleaning 94–95, 149

Tack room 94

Tacking up 82–91

T'ai chi 144

Teeth 86, 93

Titbits 16

Transitions 100, 102, 104, 105, 108

TREC 185

Trotting 63–67, 100, 104, 108, 124
  poles 124
  without stirrups 78–79

Turning a horse 60

Tying up a horse 84–85, 164

Untacking 92–93

Upwards transition 108

Vetting a horse 180

Viewing a horse 179

Walking 62, 108, 124
  without stirrups 72

Walking on 58

Water 163, 175
  hemlock 160

Weeds 17, 158

Weight distribution 29, 47, 51, 152, 154

Whips 52, 113, 114, 144–148

Wire mesh 161

Withers 50, 59, 90

Worm infestation 158

Yew 158, 160

Yoga 144